T0162598

"Glenda, your stories are heartwarming, inspirational and a touch of your wit."

Janet Lindsey, Author of Peering Through A Mist,
A Mom's Journey in Loss and God's Grace

*H*On My Way
Home

Glenda Counts Finley

WestBow
PRESS
A DIVISION OF THOMAS NELSON

WestBow Press books may be ordered through booksellers or by contacting:

WestBow Press
A Division of Thomas Nelson
1663 Liberty Drive
Bloomington, IN 47403
www.westbowpress.com
1-(866) 928-1240

Because of the dynamic nature of the Internet, any web addresses or links contained in this book may have changed since publication and may no longer be valid. The views expressed in this work are solely those of the author and do not necessarily reflect the views of the publisher, and the publisher hereby disclaims any responsibility for them.
Scripture taken from the New King James Version. Copyright 1979, 1980, 1982 by Thomas Nelson, inc. Used by permission. All rights reserved.

Scripture quotations taken from the New American Standard Bible®, Copyright © 1960, 1962, 1963, 1968, 1971, 1972, 1973, 1975, 1977, 1995 by The Lockman Foundation. Used by permission." (www.Lockman.org)

Scripture quotations taken from the Holy Bible, New Living Translation, copyright 1996, 2004. Used by permission of Tyndale House Publishers, Inc., Wheaton, Illinois 60189. All rights reserved.

Scripture taken from the Holy Bible, New International Version®. Copyright © 1973, 1978, 1984 Biblica. Used by permission of Zondervan. All rights reserved.

Scripture taken from the King James Version of the Bible.

Author photo taken by Jennifer Householder

ISBN: 978-1-4497-6076-2 (sc)
Library of Congress Control Number: 2012914517

Printed in the United States of America
WestBow Press rev. date: 05/30/2013

For my glorious daughters,
Amanda and Jennifer
And my beloved mother, Jean
And my wonderful husband, Rod
And my favorite sons-in-law,
Robbie and Parker
And last and really the least,
My extremely precious granddaughter, Caroline

You are all the loves of my life.

May God always bless you with joy!

*You should rejoice at a death
and cry at a birth.*

*"And the day of one's death is better than
the day of one's birth." Ecclesiastes 7:1*

Preface

As I READ THROUGH my dear friend, Janet Lindsey's book Peering Through A Mist, I kept anticipating the part about the flowers I had brought for her at the lake. But when I had finished the book and the story wasn't there, I have to admit I was somewhat disappointed.

Then as I prayed about my whiny condition, God helped me to realize that the story about the flowers wasn't just for Janet but was just as much for me. He led me to realize that if I wanted the story shared, then I should write it down.

And when I began making notes, He reminded me of a few other stories that I wanted to share with my children and pass on down to my grandchildren. Before I knew it there were over a dozen stories that I really wanted to share with my family and friends. And the list just kept growing.

Each story, although some seem unbelievable, is absolutely true. And during the final editing He even gave me a couple more stories to add. So even though "my story" is far from over, my book is complete.

I hope you enjoy reading it. I know my family is truly appreciative of the fact that I wrote this book instead of telling all of these stories… they already think I talk too much!

Acknowledgements

*T*HANK YOU JESUS FOR saving me. Thank You for my family and friends. Thank You for always providing me the most wondrous gifts on earth. Thank You especially for Your Promise of eternity in Heaven with You. And thank You for this laptop so I didn't have to use a hammer and chisel!

Thanks to my family and friends who have always been such a great inspiration to me. And although they didn't know of my classified, top-secret mission, they have helped me tremendously. Except there should be a special thanks to Jennifer who figured out my privileged information, your encouragement and photography skills meant volumes!

Thanks to Janet who painstakingly read through my rough drafts. Your help was enormous. And your courage to write in the midst of the darkest storm of your life has been instrumental in my new venture. Words could never describe what your friendship has meant to me.

And thanks to Laura and Kathy, two of my retail therapist, who found out about my assignment, "the book". You were so very supportive and I truly appreciate all of your help, book-wise and therapy-wise!

Again, thanks to all my family and friends. If I didn't mention you by name it's only because you were not privy to the classified information. And a great big thanks to whoever added a thesaurus to computers, I could never have done this without it!

Contents

Born in a Barn

SHE WAS A YOUNG, teenage girl out wandering in the wilderness. When it started to rain, she hurried into a nearby barn to seek shelter from the storm. Once inside she saw that there was a huge pile of hay just harvested. So she climbed and climbed until she had reached the top.

The view from so high allowed her to see the entire barn as she had never seen it before. She could look straight down into the corn-crib where her Grandpa had shown her the feed, hay rakes and rope. And although she knew he had told her to never be in the barn during the storm, she reasoned that it was only raining and she was dry here.

But then as she surveyed the rest of the barn, her gaze brought her to the stalls where they kept the animals. The one just below her withheld a cattle trough she realized she had never really noticed before. God began to reveal Himself to her by opening her eyes to see that this trough was much like the one where the newborn Baby Jesus was laid. It was not clean or disinfected or even well-sanded.

She envisioned the animals eating from it with their drool. No one had cleaned or sterilized that manger where the actual Creator of the world was born to earth. The floor of the stall was dirt with the smell of animals and although she knew that Mary and Joseph had done everything they could, it was still just a barn.

1

It was still just a dirty, old barn. She, at that moment, realized for the first time that the very King of Kings had left all the royalty and purity of Heaven to be born in the most dismal of all circumstances... for her...to be her Savior.

As the tears began to flow, she noticed there was one corner post of the stall that was much larger than the other. Her eyes followed it up, up to the ceiling. But before it reached the ceiling, it crossed a main support beam for the roof of the barn.

Staring her in the face, at eye level, was an enormous cross. The wood was all too real and she knew its rough exterior from the many splitters she had suffered through the years. And there were bugs crawling on it.

She had never thought or let herself know that there were possibly bugs crawling on Jesus. As His back was against that rough, wooden cross, tearing even more flesh away from His already mangled skin, there were flies buzzing Him. There were possibly spiders crawling over the wood...over His body.

Then as her eyes caught sight of the old rusty nail protruding from the beam, she looked down at her own palm. For she knew too well of the nails that were driven into the very hands of the Creator. She knew that Jesus had been nailed to that old wooden cross with spikes even larger than the spears that were piercing the wood she now faced.

Her head fell into her hands as she wept. She began to beg for His forgiveness for all her sins that had caused Him so much pain. She began to plead for Him to forgive her. She prayed to ask Him to be her Savior. She prayed that although she didn't understand what it meant, that she would follow Him for the rest of her life. She prayed that He would be the Lord of her life. And she trusted Him to direct her.

When she raised her head, although she did not understand it all, she did know that she had walked into this barn a lost sinner. And she had now been born into the kingdom of God. She was now a child of The King. She knew that she was now promised an eternity in Heaven. And no one, no way, no how could ever pluck her from her Father's Hands. She was so secure in her salvation.

In fact, she was so secure, that she had not even noticed that the rain shower had turned into a major thunderstorm, a storm that normally she would be trembling to hear. A thunderstorm that was so intense that it was extremely loud and demanded the attention of everyone.

She then realized that she was sitting on the top of a huge pile of hay in her Grandpa's barn. The very barn he had warned her to never be in during a storm. The very barn where he had shown her the trails of the lightning strikes from the large old oak tree leading directly to the barn. He had cautioned her that if the lightning were to strike the barn or one of the nearby trees, the barn could burn within a few seconds.

And now here she sat. She was sitting in the most dangerous place she had possibly ever sat. With the lightning flashing through the sky and the gigantic crashes of thunder, she was oddly at total peace. There was such a peace and a calm she had never known before. She felt strangely secure as if sitting in the very Hand of God, as if He was holding her in the palms of His Hands. And there was nothing that could harm her, could ever harm her.

She knew without a doubt that if lightning were to strike her directly and she were to die instantly, she would not die. For now she would live forever. Only her body could be touched by death. She for the first time in her life had no fear of death. Death was not her enemy, for Jesus had conquered death. And she was now secure in her relationship with Him.

She knew that on this day of her life, like Jesus, she had, for all eternity, been born in a barn.

Yes, I was born in a barn.

Jesus answered and said to him, "Most assuredly, I say to you, unless one is born again, he cannot see the kingdom of God." John 3:3 NKJV

What God Wants

*A*s I SAT ON the wall along the sidewalk outside my college class, I had my head down. With the book opened and my long hair on each side of my face, I hoped no one would notice that my eyes were closed. I was hoping no one would know I was talking to God, questioning whether I was doing anything right. *"Oh God, am I doing anything You want me to do?"*

It had started on Saturday night at work. I had been working the cash register when a man came in and proceeded to try to scam me out of some cash. But having seen the news report just the night before of how these scams worked, I knew I had to pay close attention.

The scammers try to have bills changed back and forth until you are so confused you believe them and give them back more than they are due. It was very tense but in the end he said I owed him twenty dollars. I politely but firmly told him, "No sir, I do not." Although he tried to convince me, I knew I had kept up with it and was correct.

Almost as soon as the scammer had left, a very eccentric looking gentleman walked in. Once I had taken his order and told him his balance due, he told me he did not have to pay. "What do you mean you don't have to pay?" I asked rather sternly.

No he didn't have to pay, he began to explain, because he was one of the owners. "Well, who are you?" I asked quite harshly. After explaining and my verifying he was who he said, I think I felt my knees buckle a little bit. He not only was one of the owners, he knew my father. And was Daddy's boss!

A few minutes later I was waiting on a customer whose daughter was with her. The daughter was so extremely deformed and disabled that my heart began to break. She was blind and deaf and her face was disfigured. I totally felt ashamed that I had ever complained about anything. This was not a normal night at the local fast food restaurant.

I left work feeling overwhelmed and defeated. But after a somewhat restless night's sleep, I hurried off to church the next morning to teach my five year old Sunday school class of ten children. However, on this day everything seemed to go wrong.

First the felt board people wouldn't stick to the felt board during story time. And all of the children seemed squirmier than usual. Then we went over for craft time and that's when the real fun began.

Stephen, who was a handful all by himself, was painting the front of one of the little girl's dresses. Nice big strokes up and down. He was immediately sent to the time out chair. But as would be expected, he casually sauntered over that way as I rushed over to take the little girl to the bathroom next door to try to wash out the paint before it set in.

Of course this wasn't any little girl's dress, I thought as I frantically tried to get all the paint out. It had to be the perfect little girl. The one who was always dressed perfect and always acted perfect. And I'm pretty sure that her parents were perfect too and had never had a hair out of place.

She really was like a little angel. And I'm fairly certain we should never paint on an angel.

Finally with the stain washed out and only a huge wet blob on the front of her dress, we hurried back over to the classroom to finish up before the bell. Unfortunately, the bell rang as I was opening the classroom door. I only hoped that its clanging drowned out my screams.

For there was Stephen who ran across the room, leaped onto the bookshelf, ran across it, back to the floor, up on a chair, and then to the piano bench. From there he jumped up onto the keyboard of the piano where he proceeded to run up and down the keys. After that it's just a blur.

Parents were coming in and out to get their children while scratching their heads and mumbling as they left. Of course Stephen's brother came to get him but did take time to ask if there was something wrong.

Once I had explained, he drug Stephen off as only a brother can do and sent his father back to talk with me. Having told him of what had happened, it appeared that steam began to come out of his ears. I'm not exactly sure what happened to Stephen when they got home but after that you couldn't have asked for a better child.

However, as for that day my nerves were frazzled. So coming to my class this morning I was already feeling like my life was headed in the wrong direction. I was already questioning everything I was doing. And to top the last two days off, I got the exam back from last week and I had failed!

Failed – really? This was my major. How could I fail this exam? I know any one of these things must seem like no big deal but to a student who is trying to find their way in the world it was devastating.

As I hung my head, I began to ask God if I was doing anything right. Am I in the right major? Am I working where I should be? Do you really want me to keep teaching this Sunday school class?

It was then that I started to understand why some students could become so distraught that they would jump off the bridge. I pleaded to God to help me to know. I wasn't suicidal myself, but I needed answers. Answers to "Am I doing anything You want me to do?"

It was at that moment that I felt someone tap me on the shoulder. I raised my head to see a girl had sat next to me on the wall. She asked if I minded if she asks me some questions. Her first question was, "Do you know Jesus Christ as your personal Savior?" I told her I did and that answer in and of itself was so comforting. Yes I do know Jesus!

Then she asked if I went to church and where. And how was I involved in my church. I told her about the Sunday school class and the other activities I was doing at the time.

Next was did I work and then about my major. I explained both and just telling what I did somehow made those things seem a little more important…to somebody anyway.

Then as she stood up to leave she said the strangest thing. She said, "Well it sounds like you are doing exactly what God wants you to do. Keep up the good work."

I glanced back down at my book. Did she just say what I think she said? I looked back up to see if this girl was for real or if she had earned her wings and taken flight. But she was gone. She was nowhere in sight.

God had sent me a messenger; a messenger to answer my question to the tee. I feel sure she is still wondering why in the world she said that.

But I guess she was doing exactly what God wanted her to do too!

Christmas Peace

*M*Y GRANDMA LIVED NEXT door so I would walk the old farm road to her house anytime I wanted. After I turned sixteen, I took her to the grocery store, doctor's office, church or wherever she needed to go.

Once when I dropped in she called me into the dining room. She climbed up on a little stool and reached back in behind all the stuff on the top shelf.

Out she pulled a crystal, basket-shaped flower vase. She told me she wanted me to have it but to not tell any of the other grandkids. I always giggle to myself when I think about it now.

She had never given me anything before except for maybe a five dollar bill at Christmas or for my birthday. She would have it folded and would slip it into the palm of my hand and whisper, "Don't tell any of the other grandkids."

Then she told me that my Grandpa's mother had owned the vase when she and Grandpa were first married. Grandma had told her that she liked it, so my great-grandmother had given it to my Grandma. And now she was giving it to me. A priceless treasure from my Grandma to always cherish.

As I was standing there in the cold December night on that Christmas Eve, the twinkle of the stars reminded me of the glistening flowers on the front of that vase. Grandma was now in the hospital where she had been for over a month. She had suffered a heart attack.

After my aunt had called me I was the first to get to the hospital and was the first to get to go in to see her. She looked so weak and pale lying in that bed.

I had now been visiting her for weeks and kept asking her what she wanted for Christmas. She had never been a big one for gifts but I enjoyed throwing out temptations. She was so weak she could barely talk. Each time I would go through a list of items that would always end with a teddy bear.

Now I am sure she never owned a teddy bear. And I know grown people don't really need teddy bears. But it always made her smile a little childish grin that I will cherish forever. It was just one more of our little secrets. Then on the day before Christmas Eve when I asked her, she said in a low, raspy voice, "I want to go home."

My aunt over in the corner looked up from her newspaper and responded, "Oh Momma, you know that's impossible. You know you can't go home."

My Grandma looked at me with all the reassurance that she knew that she could go home. I didn't really understand what she was talking about at the time. So I said that I believed in miracles and that I thought anything was possible. I squeezed her hand. And with a grin, a nod and a weary wink, she mouthed the words, "Go home."

So there I stood overlooking the city on that cold, Christmas Eve while my fiancé was inside spreading a little Christmas cheer. Our plans were to go on to the hospital from there and meet up with the rest of my family. We were going to take Grandma her gifts and spend some time with her for the evening.

Then my friend stuck her head out the door to tell me that my mother had called and said I should come straight home. I knew what that meant.

A sudden numbness engulfed my body. But as I turned back to look out over the sparkling lights of the city, there was a calm. Then, looking skyward into the twinkling stars of Heaven, pure peace.

This was Christmas Peace! The Peace that passes all understanding. Jesus Christ had come to this world some two thousand years ago so that on this very night, this very Christmas night, my Grandma could…

go home!

"Trust Me"

*H*AVING LIVED IN A small rental house for the past seven years was just one of the driving factors behind me wanting a home of our own. But wanting to be out of town, with a big yard for my daughter to play outside was the biggest part of it.

And I wanted to be able to paint the walls whatever color I wanted. And I wanted to be out of the city. I wanted a place where we could invite over friends or have the youth from church over. Where I could feel the presence of God; and not listen for the sounds of gunshots. Pretty much the same thing everybody wants with a new house.

So I began to pray that God would lead us to a new house. Not necessarily brand new, but new for us. Knowing our finances, I started back to work full-time. And how I found the job was a miracle of sorts in itself.

I mentioned to my husband Rod that I was thinking about going back to work since our daughter was now two and I knew we needed the extra income. I hoped to save most of what I made to put toward a down payment. And since grandparents were willing to babysit most of the time it sounded like a good plan. So we headed off to play cards with friends.

Now I don't want to say that my mouth flew open or anything, but I was surprised when my friend asked soon after we had arrived if we knew of anyone who was looking for a job. It hadn't even been an hour since I had talked to Rod about it. And God had already got me a lead!

I told her yes, called the man first thing Monday morning and went by for the interview that afternoon. He asked me when I could start. I told him immediately so I started right then and there.

The job was only temporary but they soon offered me a full-time position. And it was close to my parents and in-laws so my babysitters were just minutes away.

I worked and saved and yes dreamed too for the new house we could someday own. And even started scouting out the neighborhoods for anything that might look promising.

When we thought we were getting close to being ready, we contacted a realtor we knew for help to know our limitations. And the search was on. He told us that if we would be patient that he would stay with us and keep looking until we found exactly what we were looking for.

We went out almost weekly for months, going through house after house. Until one afternoon as we were on our way to look at another house, I pointed to a house I liked just beyond an empty lot. I told him that if he could get me a house just like that one, it would be perfect.

"Well I just heard that house might be going on the market soon. If you would like for me to check, we may be able to get in to see it before it's listed with a realtor," he said.

The next day we were in the car again headed to the house I loved. "A very strange thing happened when I called to see if we could come to see the house," he said. "It seems the people who own the house have the very same last name as you."

Rod and I looked at each other in a puzzled, disbelief. When he told us their first names, we realized it was my husband's uncle and aunt! By then we were pulling in the driveway and walking up the steps of the front porch.

As she flung open the door, Rod's aunt was a little more stunned than us and couldn't stop talking. After a tour of the house, I was in love with it. Then when they told us what they would ask us to pay for it, it was thousands of dollars less than the tax appraisal. Less than we had planned to pay! And less than it was worth!

Their reasoning was that the tax appraisal was too high, the realtor disagreed. And they needed to be able to live there until they could get another house built. So we set to work getting ready to make the purchase and close on the house.

But right before we were to close, my employer received word that one of the major lines we carried was being pulled. We would no longer carry any of those products which accounted for some eighty percent of our earnings. I ran all the figures I could and knew there was no way to stay in business without that line.

So I started calculating our personal expenses without my salary. There was no way. No matter how I tried there was just no way to make the numbers add up.

What was I supposed to do? Do I go ahead and get the house knowing that in a matter of months we wouldn't be able to make the payments? Or do I tell Rod we are going to have to back out on the deal?

But God had led me to that house. As I left and headed to the bank to make a deposit for work, I began to pray.

I asked God all the questions that had been running through my head. I reminded Him of all the numbers I had ran and how things just wouldn't add up. My words were racing frantically as I tried to justify in some way what rationale anyone would have for going ahead and buying the house.

"Trust Me" came a clear, strong voice. The words interrupted my unrelenting questions and seemed to echo throughout the car with an uncommon familiarity.

I immediately jerked my head around to see who was in the backseat. Then I looked at the radio but it was turned off. I peered out the windows for any cars, anyone who could have audibly said these words. But there was no one. There was no one to make any kind of noise. There was no one to verify that they heard the words too.

The words stopped me like a ton of bricks. Not stopped the car, but stopped my mind from this endless race against rationality.

"Oh God! Was that You God?" Peace filled the car and surrounded me like a well-worn glove.

Trust God? That seemed so simple and although it didn't add up, it only seemed right. *"Yes, I will trust You, O God. I will trust You as best I can. But I won't deny it, I will need help. I'm very weak and You know I will have my times of doubt. Please help me in those times."*

That night at home I wanted to make sure that what God had told me truly lined up with His Word. Not that I doubted God but I doubted me. Was there some way I had created this in my head? I don't know how. The voice actually interrupted me in my ramblings. And I heard it with my ears and not just in my head. The voice actually came from outside my head.

I sat down with my Bible and began looking at all the places God had used the word trust or conveyed the idea that we should trust Him. I soon realized that the entire Bible is truly telling us to trust God.

It started 'In the beginning' when God told Adam not to eat the fruit, "Trust Me". And Noah was told to build an ark, really? With not a drop of rain in sight, "Trust Me". And Moses, "Go get My people out of Egypt." Who me? "Trust Me". And Abraham, and David, and Daniel, and Isaiah, right up to Mary and Joseph, "Trust Me".

Jesus entire message was to trust Him. And the message of all those who followed Jesus was to trust Jesus Christ as their personal Savior and to trust Him daily as Lord. From the very first letter of Genesis to the very last period of Revelation, God has been saying to me, to everyone, "Trust Me".

I don't know how I could have been so stupid. The first thing I had done when I had a problem was to try to take it on myself. I had tried to figure it out. I was trying to fix it when all along I had the Creator of the universe, my Savior, my Father, my dearest Friend, just waiting for me to call out to Him. Just waiting for me to bring Him my every care. Just waiting to bless me with His Presence. Just waiting for me to start trusting Him…with everything.

We went ahead and bought the house with me knowing in just a few short months my work would go under. And I would be out of a job. All the income we had planned to go toward the house payments just wouldn't exist. Still I didn't tell my husband of what was to come but kept silently trusting God.

I worked a little over a month after we moved before my boss came to me and asked if he should remain opened. I explained he was losing money every day and there seemed to be no hope. So we turned off the phones and locked the doors right then and there.

I worked through the end of the week cleaning up, closing the books and clearing out everything. He generously paid me an additional two weeks compensation. And by the time that ran out, my husband had received a quite sizable promotion that almost made up more than half my salary!

Over the next ten years we lived there, God continually poured out His blessings on our family. Every time we were in a pinch, I would go to Him and pray. I would remind Him that He told me to trust Him and that I was having a hard time.

Sometimes I would get called in to work a fill-in position I worked whenever someone was out sick or was on maternity leave. Those calls always came at exactly the right time.

One time we were coming up short one hundred eighty dollars on the house payment when we received a check in the mail for one hundred eighty-nine dollars. It was a refund on our insurance. We didn't even know we were due a refund!

"Thank You God for allowing me to hear Your Voice. Thank You for teaching me to trust You."

"Trust in the Lord, and do good; Dwell in the land, and feed on His faithfulness." Psalm 37:3 NKJV

My Garden

*I*THANKED GOD CONTINUALLY FOR my new home that He had given. And for my family which soon grew by one more. But in this new place, something was missing. I yearned for that time I had spent at home growing up. I truly missed all those long walks I would take out around the family farm just talking to God. It was in a sense my garden.

As I asked God to give me that time again, Rod was making changes to the back yard. I soon realized that what this new side walk and pool area needed was landscaping.

As I set to work planting flowers and later pulling weeds as the children played, I knew that this was God's answer to my prayers. All that time on my knees was a glorious time in my life. I could keep up with what my children were doing while talking to my Best Friend.

And all the aching in my knees and back was such a very small price to pay to spend time with my Lord. Weeds became my joy. For I knew that with every weed there was a moment *we* could share. I learned in that time "in all things give thanks". Yes, even weeds can be a blessing.

One day I saw a painting with bluebirds. They were so beautiful I thought how I wished we could get bluebird houses and try to attract these gorgeous creatures. Very soon afterwards as I was doing the dishes, I noticed a bluebird in our backyard. Although we had done nothing to attract them, they just started coming in our yard. Just a male and a female, but it was such a blessing to know God had supplied my need.

Psalm 23:1 tells me, "The Lord is my Shepherd; I shall not want." The dictionary describes 'want' as 'have need of'. So, I will not have need of…period. In other words, as long as I follow the Lord, I will not have need of anything!

The more time I spent with my Lord on my knees in the backyard, the more it seemed to irritate the neighbor next door. So after doing all we knew we could, we felt led to move.

We went to live in my Grandma's old house next to my parents. We planned to build a house there on the farm. I decided to let Rod choose where he wanted the house since I was so excited to be moving back to the farm.

In the meantime we put our house up for sale. It had been on the market for months when I went by to check on things. I prayed in the now empty living room that God would lead those people He wanted to live here. I prayed that He would prepare them. And that He would give the family who could best reach this neighbor. I prayed that the sale of the house could be soon. And that from wherever they needed to come, even if it was from as far away as California, that He would lead them here.

A few days later our realtor called to say she had a couple who loved the house. And they wanted to buy it, at the asking price! Thank you God!

She didn't think it would be a problem since the house was empty but they would be moving in next weekend. Well that was the plan but they had to go home first. And have the movers pack them and then drive back here…from California. God is so good!

We had the exterior finished on our new house and just the finishing work inside was left. The carpenter, who was working on the fireplace mantle and stairs, was inside working. And the site foreman was in the garage cutting the trim for the cabinets.

I had arrived suffering from dream-house-construction-stress-syndrome, or that's what I called it, after just getting off the phone with our contractor. Anybody who says building a house is not stressful has either never built a house or is delirious.

But when I got out of the car to go inside, the foreman had his radio playing to one of my favorite Christian praise songs. It was refreshing. Then when I went through the door into the house, the carpenter inside had his radio tuned to the same song.

I paused to thank God, *"Thank You Dear Lord. You always bless me when I am here."*

"Isn't that what you asked for?"

A sudden rush of memories of a time some twenty-four or so years ago flooded into my mind. A time when I had spent countless hours at this very spot on one of my walks and talks with God.

I would walk the farm talking and listening to God. But regardless of which direction I started out walking, it seemed I would always end up here. Sitting under the trees on top of this hill, I could see down to both my parents' house and to my grandparents' house.

So I would sit here until we were both comfortable with just sharing each other's company. Until I knew once again that peace that only God can give. Once again that peace that passes all understanding.

But God brought back to my memory the prayer I had prayed on that one particular day about this place. I had prayed that God would give me forever this place.

And that I would always have the opportunity to come here. That He would give me whatever I needed here to have this time with Him. Regardless of whether it was the size of a cemetery plot or half an acre or even five acres, I prayed that God would give me whatever I needed to have my garden.

We had told my father that all we needed for the house was half an acre, but he had insisted. So we were deeded five acres!

There were bluebirds too that were always outside our bedroom window. And there were not just two bluebirds, but many times there were more than I could count.

I know that all of this was not just a coincidence. But instead a bad neighbor was an instrument used by God to get me back to...

my garden.

Westward Bound!

*A*s we cruised down the interstate, praying and searching frantically for a dealership, I thought back to my first trip out west. This was supposed to be that way too. But this was not what I remembered at all.

It actually started twenty-five years before in January when my father had first mentioned a trip out west. He told us he was planning on quitting his job which was by all accounts sucking the life out of him and our family. And how would we like to take a vacation out west for the summer. A vacation not to see so much of the man-made world but to see more of what God had made.

I was somewhat hesitant since I had just started dating and couldn't see that being gone all summer was of any great benefit to me. But knowing how excited my father was and how he needed to leave his current job, I jumped on board.

We spent the winter gathered around the table with maps and brochures planning our great adventure. He quit in May and we left mid-June for our nine week journey. The trunk of our Pontiac loaded with two pup tents, four sleeping bags, four air mattresses, an ice chest and more clothes than we ever needed, we headed off westward bound.

We had our route carefully planned and would stop each night to camp. The trip was practically perfect. No mishaps and the weather was impeccable. But the best of all was that I got my daddy back.

The man that had been over-worked, over-stressed and exhausted was now relaxed, fun and tireless.

The trip had been so wonderful for me that I said I would love to be able to do the same thing with my own family someday. Not just for a trip out west but to even better show my family this Majestic, Wonderful God I had grown to love so dearly. But now that I was older with children of my own, I could never see how a trip out west might be possible.

Then, amazingly, when our house was almost finished, the company where my husband had worked for twenty-three years closed. That was a horrible loss in our life. But its closing had compensated employees who had agreed to stay until the end with sizable severance packages.

My husband's package was more than a year's salary so my father suggested we take their motorhome out west for the summer. Rod would have never agreed to go in tents therefore God had really made the way possible. I prayed that through this trip, my family could see how great God truly is.

So here we were on the second day of our trip. Just now getting out to where none of my family had ever been before, we had stopped for gas. But the motor home had died when we stopped and wouldn't start again. After finally getting it across the street to a shop, we were told we needed to take it to a dealership in St. Louis.

Driving another thirty miles to the city, we had no idea where to find a dealership nor what we were going to do if it had to be left in the shop overnight. To our amazement we saw the dealership on the right of the interstate as we were approaching the exit.

I prayed that we would be able to get a green light so as not to have to stop before we reached the garage doors. Slowing down as we made our approach, the light turned green! The next turn had a yielding merge lane but there was nothing coming, no cars in sight. We slowly made each turn and parked right in front of the garage bay doors.

The dealership took us first to the hotel across the street to get a room. Then they drove Rod down the street to get a rental car to drive around town. We got to tour the St. Louis Arch, continue our trip and didn't miss a beat!

By the time we had finished touring the city, the motor home was done and ready to go. This was our first chance to praise God for taking care of our family.

The second chance came sooner than we would have liked. As we headed on west, we got a tank of bad gas and started having problems again. We were pulled off on the side of the interstate when a police officer stopped to assist us. He led us off the interstate back to a gas station because we had failed to hear the weather report that there was a tornado coming...straight toward us!

We got out and went into the building amidst flying sand and gravel just in time to find the staff sending everyone to the basement. Before we made it to the basement door, however, the power went out. Once downstairs we found ourselves standing in the dark in a room full of strangers on a dirt floor with only a couple of flashlights.

As we directed the lights up the shelves on the walls of the small basement, we realized the shelves were lined with buffalo skulls. So here we stood in the dark with the thunderous roar of the tornado passing overhead, buffalo skulls surrounding us on the walls and mud-puddles at our feet. And again I say, "God is so good!"

The tornado followed the path of the interstate for several miles coming right past the station. The enormous sign for the gas station had been taken some fifty feet but our family had been safe. We were definitely seeing how great God truly is!

Another day we were coming out of a restaurant as there were tornado sirens going off. As we looked across the horizon, we could see the tornado moving across the path we had planned to take.

Still another day during a steady, pouring bitter rain while traveling down a winding mountain canyon road, we started appreciating how important the brakes were here. The guardrail along the edge of the road was overlooking an immediate plunging gorge.

The next morning, when we got up it had snowed so much that Yellowstone was closed. Although it was extremely rare for it to snow so late in June, we decided to make the best of it. So as we drove around the town going to a rodeo and a western museum, we realized that the brakes had gone out. We were able to stay safely there in town and the repairs were completed about the time the park reopened. It seemed that God had not only protected us as we had traveled down the winding canyon road but had also provided snow to protect us from what would have inevitably been a disaster.

For soon after entering Yellowstone, my husband mentioned that he sure would like to get to see an elk up close. As we rounded the next curve, there was the biggest, broadest elk standing in the middle of the road. The brakes worked perfectly. Lots of items were instantly rearranged in the motor home, but the brakes worked great!

Then on another day we found horse riding stables at the foot of the mountains. As we were saddling up for our ride, my horse suddenly began to buck and not just a mild, quick buck. But a fully reared up on his hind legs and hold it for what seemed like forever kind of buck!

I tried to remain calm and soothe the horse to keep all four feet on the ground. As we were trying to settle down, I could hear the horse trainer explaining to Rod that my horse was a little fidgety since it was a newly caught mustang. But it was truly a privilege for me to get to ride it, he continued, because it was just like the horse Christopher Reeve was thrown from that caused him to be paralyzed. Now that's reassuring!

My horse did okay the rest of the ride. But Rod's horse, which was a huge, old Clydesdale, was almost uncontrollable. The horse definitely had a mind of his own and loved straying off the trail. He would take Rod under every low lying branch possible which I believe the horse was doing on purpose. And I never was quite sure if that old, retired police horse was snorting or chuckling.

Traveling on down the road we found a whitewater rafting trip on the Snake River. But oddly enough they had not given us any helmets. Since I was the only one who had been whitewater rafting before, no one else thought it was strange at all.

And the river was so mild I thought maybe I was just over reacting to the lack of head protection for my family. Until, however, the guide announced that we should all brace for the upcoming rapids. These were the worst ones on this part of the river, he was explaining, and was known as the "Widow-Maker."

In our positions and paddling as hard as we could, we started through the rapids. And in a split second, Rod was thrown from the raft headfirst into the raging river. All I could think was, "I don't want to be a widow!"

As he disappeared from sight, I had a tremendous fear of his sudden dive head first, with no helmet, into the river's malicious waters sending him straight into the jagged rocks so clearly beneath the water's surface. And as we scrambled to try to follow the guide's instructions, I frantically watched through teary eyes the water for that gush of blood to emerge.

But instead Rod popped up, no injuries of any kind, not thrilled but not any apparent injuries. I breathed a sigh of relief as the guide drug him back into the raft. Well actually the guide shoved him underwater to get a jump start from the life-jacket and pulled as Rod quite comically flopped back into the boat. And we then continued to the landing to make our exit, soppy husband and all.

So what would have seemed like an endless barrage of problems just brought our family closer together. We could never deny that without the Hand of God, we would never have survived our vacation. He had continued to show us how He had watched out over us. Our trip only lasted three weeks but I knew God had given me just one more unforgettable gift as we were –

westward bound!

Thanksgiving

WHEN I ARRIVED TO pick up my only brother, he said he wasn't going home. "What do you mean, you are not going home?"

He wouldn't tell me where he was going, but he got in the car with some friends and drove off. He and my father had a falling out before he left for his trip. And now I was sent to pick him up when he had returned. What was I going to do?

My parents were devastated. What had been intended as a disciplinary action, a simple grounding after his trip, had blown up in their faces. We couldn't find out where he had gone or who he was staying with. And since he was over eighteen, the police department couldn't help us.

I had to watch my parents go from active, vibrant, healthy, middle-aged adults to hollow, slumped, withered, aged shells of human beings. They were constantly crying and depressed and there seemed to be nowhere to turn. All efforts to make contact with my brother just seemed to bring more hurt.

And although I tried to help them as much as possible, I soon realized that there was nothing I could say or do. As days turned into months and months turned into years, I slowly but assuredly began to realize that for all practical purposes…I was an only child.

Thanksgiving was my first realization of what our new life was going to be like. As we gathered to sit down for dinner, my father looked like death. His body seemed frail and he looked like he had been tortured for months, reminding me of pictures of the Jews during the Holocaust. My mother wasn't much better. But she still had some hope that my brother would come home for the holiday dinner. The entire day was desperately mournful there with my shriveled, withered family.

Sitting down to eat this wonderful meal of tasteful delicacies, food just seemed to make a huge lump in my throat that was extremely hard to swallow. It is very hard to act hungry when you actually feel nauseous. Regardless of how hard I tried to make the day somewhat pleasant, I felt I was a horrible failure. It was a feeling that would stick with me for years to come.

But that was just the first bad Thanksgiving of many to come. No holiday was ever the same, for there was always an empty chair at the table. There was always that anxiety over whether this would be the year that he would decide to come home. Years and years of waiting…waiting and wondering.

I anguished over the hurt I saw in my parents. That first Mother's Day was heart-breaking. But the first Father's Day was even more gut-wrenching.

I cried out to God, *"Please, oh God! Please bring my brother home. Oh God, how long will we have to suffer this anguish? What will it take to get my brother to come home? How long will it be before he returns?"*

The answer soon came during church one Sunday evening, just as clearly as looking through a cool mountain stream. ***"Twenty-one years."***

"What do you mean, twenty-one years?" I questioned with great anticipation. Could God seriously be telling me it would take twenty-one years for my brother to come back home? Was that twenty-one years from now? Or twenty-one years from a year ago when he had originally left?

God never made it clear to me what He meant but instead expected me to trust Him. Trust Him to take care of me and my family. Trust Him to return my brother home…in His time.

Finally, God gave us a Thanksgiving that we could truly celebrate. My first daughter, Amanda, was born just a few weeks before the holiday. And since I'd had surgery, we stayed with my parents until Thanksgiving Day.

My daughter was the beginning of life for our family. Our family was finally reborn. And my second daughter, Jennifer, just increased the joy and gave my parents more reason to want to live.

And so we were finally a family again. But through holidays, illnesses and hospital stays, I continued to be an only child. I continued to carry the weight of caring for my parents. I was alone in "Honor your father and your mother" Exodus 20:12 NKJV.

Until another Thanksgiving when I knew that my parents were soon to be separated. Not just separated from each other, but separated from our family and from the world.

As I pulled out my chair to sit down for dinner, I was consumed with the reality that this was my last Thanksgiving with my father. I felt drenched in the foresight of his upcoming death. Glancing over at him already seated next to me, the feeling overwhelmed me and seemed to devour my every fiber. He looked okay, but I knew in my heart that Daddy would not be here next year. And that my brother would be. My brother would finally return to take his seat at the family table.

I thought I was going to choke. I wanted to savor every moment we had left together. I wanted to absorb like a good sponge every bit of my father here with my new family. I wanted to set life in slow motion, to push pause and freeze this frame in my mind.

My father had been diagnosed a few months earlier with Myelodysplastic Syndrome. The same thing two of his brothers had dealt with before getting cancer and dying. And although people don't die from this syndrome, it is normally a precursor to cancer, specifically leukemia. But he was doing fine with his MDS and it hadn't shown any signs of progressing to leukemia.

Still there was that haunting feeling, that feeling of death creeping into our family. That feeling that I knew would take my father whom I had grown so much closer to over the past years.

We had finally developed a relationship where I felt like I could really talk to him. I had worked with him. And I had ridden to and from work with him which allowed us a lot of time to talk, a lot of time that I would now cherish for the rest of my life. And there were those numerous days I had driven over to meet him for lunch before he retired. Now these would be some of my favorite, most momentous lunch memories.

Then, unfortunately but not to my surprise, about a month later my father was diagnosed with Acute Myelogenous Leukemia. He battled the cancer for some seven months. My mother always stayed with him at the hospital. And although often difficult while working full-time fifty minutes away, I made it a point to try to go visit him every day he was in the hospital.

He died on the twenty-first day of July. My brother came to the funeral. My heart broke.

But a few months later it was Thanksgiving again. Then as we sat down to eat, my mind raced back to that last Thanksgiving. My sense of dread and of impending doom had come full circle and was now realized. I couldn't help but agonize over the huge emptiness in the room.

My brother was there, along with his wife and children. And still yet, my heart was breaking. I think I cried through the entire meal. Was this really what I had to give to have my brother come back home?

Thinking back over the years, the time between my prayers begging for my brother to come back home until then had been exactly twenty-one years. Twenty-one years precisely as God had told me as I sat in that warm church pew worshiping Him on that piercing, bitter night.

And I am just now starting to recover from that first Thanksgiving.

"To everything there is a season, a time for every purpose under heaven." Ecclesiastes 3:1 NKJV

Life Lessons

*G*OD HAS ALWAYS SEEMED to be teaching me something, some new life lesson that is beyond my wildest dream. He is so very patient with me as sometimes He knows that I am a slow learner. And then other times He teaches me with one easy lesson.

My father was a good teacher. He didn't teach professionally. But all who worked with him said that if he told you to do something a certain way, it was because he knew, it was tried and tested, and it was the best way. With me he seemed to point me in the right direction and then stepped back to let me test the waters on my own.

One day he was out on the farm working on the fences. When I went down to take him something to eat and fresh water, he simply told me, "See that car over there? Drive it back and forth in this field."

I was fifteen almost sixteen and could barely drive an automatic but this was a stick shift! He explained the clutch and the gears. And then he told me to drive the car from one end of the field to the other. And then back.

"For how long?" I questioned.

"Until I tell you to stop," he replied.

It was a wonderful lesson. He was there if I needed him but I was alone in the car, alone with my frustration. It took away all the stress of having that parent riding along with your already nervous self. It was an absolutely wonderful driving lesson.

Daddy showing me the world.

However my Heavenly Father is the perfect Teacher. He has constantly reminded me of those lessons He has set for me in His Word.

"In everything give thanks", from I Thessalonians 5:18 NKJV, is one of my favorites. How could I not thank the Giver for His gifts?

And that was the question I was facing for my family. We weren't thanking God for the food He had supplied us. And not saying the blessing became a burden to me. I could say the blessing when I was alone and did at work while everyone else chattered on. But my yearning was for our family to offer thanks before each meal. How else could we "in everything give thanks"?

So I prayed that Rod would feel led to start insisting we say the blessing. After all he was the spiritual leader of our family. And

I thought God could just give Rod a special sermon or tell him straight out or something.

But that wasn't the way God chose to work. He knew what would not only reach Rod but would reach our parents as well. So He chose to work through a child, my daughter Jennifer to be precise.

After a lesson in Sunday school she came to lunch and announced that we couldn't eat anything until we had said the blessing. No one could argue with this adorable, little three year old so she said the blessing. But then at supper that night, she thought we should say the blessing again. So we did.

And she didn't stop. Every meal no matter where we were or who we were with, she insisted that we first say the blessing. And sometimes she even directed who should lead the blessing as well.

My Momma and Daddy couldn't argue with their precious Jennifer even if they were in a restaurant. And Rod's father, Papaw, said it was about time because his father had never allowed anyone to touch any food until the blessing had been said.

One time in a restaurant, a waiter came over to say that he appreciated seeing a family thank God for their meal. He said he had worked there for years and had never seen a family say thanks before. I thought that was rather strange considering we lived in the "Bible Belt".

But upon my own reflection I realized that I had only seen one elderly couple ask the blessing in a restaurant myself. And I had been eating out for at least thirty years. However, since then there has been a steady increase in the number of people I have noticed who are asking the blessing in restaurants. So while I thought I was learning "in everything give thanks", actually in reality I learned "a little child shall lead them" as well.

And then there was the day I lost my earring. It was one that Rod had given me one Christmas several years before. There were seven small diamonds set in gold studs and were my favorites. I wore them all the time and seldom even took them out.

But on this day I had been several places and felt sure I was still wearing them when I got home. And then I had lain down to take a nap. After the nap while looking in the mirror I noticed one of the earrings was gone.

I searched the bed where I had taken the nap but no earring. So I searched the carpet and the car and everywhere I had been in the house, still no earring. It was sickening but the earring seemed to be lost forever.

I began to pray about the earring. I prayed that God would lead me to it. I prayed that He would allow me to find it. I prayed that it would turn up somewhere but still no earring.

After several days of looking and praying I had finally come to grips with the fact that the earring was gone for good. So my prayers about the earring changed.

Instead of praying that I would find the earring, I prayed for whoever did find it to be blessed. I prayed that they would have a true appreciation for the earring and not just cast it off as a trinket. I prayed more than anything that in finding the earring, God would be glorified; that because they had found the earring, they would praise the Lord.

A few days later my prayers were answered. The earring was found and it was found by someone who truly praised God at first sight of it. God was glorified. He had given the earring to someone who had a truer appreciation for it than anyone else could possibly have... me.

As I was doing the laundry, down two-thirds through the hamper, there was the earring. I could never explain how it had gotten there. The clothes I had been wearing were not in the hamper. And I hadn't washed the quilt I was laying on for the nap yet either.

So how did the earring get there? The only explanation was that God had placed it there. God had answered my prayer so that He could be glorified.

> ***"Seek first the kingdom of God and His righteousness, and all these things shall be added to you."*** Matthew 6:33 NKJV

And seek I did. And ask I did on that day in the courthouse. As I stepped off the elevator with my toddler, Amanda, by my side we approached the window for the vehicle registrations. I let go of her hand for a split second to reach for the renewal form from my purse. But as soon as I did, Amanda darted back to the elevator. She had scampered in just as the door was closing. And then she was gone!

My two year old daughter was on an elevator...alone and going up inside of all places the county courthouse. The elevator stopped on the third floor as I frantically pushed the button. My heart was pounding and I begged for God to please protect my daughter.

Of course my mind was racing. And my heart was pounding and felt as if it was going to burst through my throat.

We were on the second floor at the courthouse. The jail was one floor down and the walkway to court was one floor up. And what kinds of people were on both floors could only be criminals in my own mind. All I could think was that she would run off that elevator when it stopped. And a child molester would be just waiting to grab her. Would I ever see my daughter again?

By this time I was on the elevator which I was certain was exceedingly too slow. I couldn't breathe until I knew she was okay. But my heart was about to beat right out of my chest. The elevator finally stopped and the doors crept opened. I expected to have to run out screaming for anyone to help me to find my daughter.

Instead standing calmly holding Amanda's hand with a very pleasant and understanding smile was a little old lady. She explained that she was waiting to get on the elevator when the doors had opened. And Amanda had come running off. She had realized immediately what had happened and knew that a frantic mother would soon be following after her young toddler.

So yes, "Ask, and it will be given to you..." Matthew 7:7 NASB Or was that 'she' will be given to you?

"Praise God from Whom all blessings flow. Praise Him all creatures here below. Praise Him above ye heavenly hosts. Praise Father, Son and Holy Ghost. Amen."

The more I sang the songs of praise to my glorious Lord and Savior, the more I wanted to praise Him. But something happened with my shoulder while we were building our house. My shoulder would hurt and the pain would run down my arm. Sometimes the pain would even spread up my neck.

And although pain relievers would ease the pain and therapy would cause it to subside, nothing seemed to completely alleviate the pain. The pain was a constant and would only vary from mild to intense.

Then one day at church I realized that God expected me to praise Him through the pain. He knew that it would have been easy for anyone to praise Him when everything was perfect. And now I didn't feel like I had been giving Him all of my praise when I was well and had no pain.

And although my shoulder was hurting so badly, I lifted my hand to Him in praise. I wanted to give Him all of me. I wanted to praise Him despite the pain. Praise Him through the pain.

And somehow, my shoulder felt slightly relieved. And although I had never been one to lift my hands in praise, nor was anyone in my church, I knew that I had praised Him just as He wanted.

I promised Him that from then on I would lift my hands in praise every time He directed me. Regardless of where I was, I would lift my hands in praise. And with that I found that the more I lifted my hand in praise, the less my shoulder would hurt. Until eventually all the pain was gone. The pain returns periodically, but my praise for Him is the constant.

And now, I lift my hands in praise in my house or in the car or when in prayer. Sometimes words just aren't enough to lift up to an Awesome, Almighty God. So why would I not want to reach my arms up to embrace my Lord?

With having traveled a lot during my life plus having worked inside the national park, I have grown to realize that nature is our evidence of the Glory of God. There have been so many times I have had to praise God for the incredible, inspiring beauty of His creation.

On one certain instance, I felt His creation was praising Him as well. Driving down one particular street on my way to work then was the essence of God's Glory. The flowers and trees in the spring are bursting with a wide hue of blooms. And then in the fall the trees and bushes are a supreme example of a vibrant, explosion of color.

But on this one specific morning as I drove into work, there was this one tree so brilliant with all of its branches reaching skyward. It appeared to be lifting its limbs, its arms, in an eruption of praise to its Creator. All of those dazzling branches lifted up, praising God.

I suddenly felt ashamed that God's creation was actually praising Him more than me. I lifted up my hands in praise. Thanking God. Praising Him.

I shared later with my classmates, laughing, that, "I wasn't going to let that tree out do me!" And since then I lift my hand in praise often without even thinking. And many times I have hit my hand on the roof of the car. I think that must be God's way of reminding me that I am not home in Heaven…yet.

But I'm on my way!

The question I was answering on the staff bio form wanted to know what my dream vacation would be. That one was easy, Hawaii! And even though I had been there before, I so wanted to have the opportunity to have more of my family see this prime piece of God's creation.

So I'm sure my mouth flew opened when my mother asked me a few months later if I would want to go with her and my cousin Donna to Hawaii. I was ecstatic and could hardly wait to reach my beloved island paradise. It was just one more precious gift from God.

And with knowing that it was God's leadership that had afforded me the opportunity to visit once again these beautiful islands, my prayer was that I could glorify Him. I prayed that God would give me a chance to tell this group how great He truly is. That He would give me the chance to praise Him in an undeniably miraculous way.

Soon enough as we were almost to the Pearl Harbor Memorial, the tour guide announced that we could not take any bags into the park. So since we had not known to be prepared, we were forced to stuff our valuables wherever we could. Most all of my money was in an exceptionally thick bank envelope I quickly stuck in the waistband of my pants since my pockets were not very deep.

At the end of the park tour, we waited in a long line to use the restroom at which point I had to take the envelope out. So I had laid it on top of the toilet paper holder. Then we went through a snack store, went out to make a few last pictures, and meandered back to the bus.

Once on the bus we began putting our things back in our purses and bags. That's when I realized it. My envelope stuffed with hundreds of dollars in twenties was gone!

I rushed off the bus muttering something about my envelope and frantically hurried across the parking lot back into the memorial park. Praying all the way, I knew that the only way the money could still be there was by an act of God. Only He could protect my cash from an enormous crowd of tourist. He was the only one who could keep this overstuffed bank envelope lying at eye level from anyone's sight.

We had stood in line to get in the park. Then we had to stand in line to take the ferry and then another line for the restroom.

All I could think was there must have been a dozen or so women in that stall since I had left. And in the privacy of the stall, who would know if they took an envelope full of cash…totally untraceable cash. And yes, I know that was a stupid thing to do!

But I quickly explained to the attendant in order to cut the line to get back in the park. And then I had to explain that I was looking for something in order to get in front of all of those ladies in line in the restroom. And of course I had to stand in front of the stall door waiting on the person inside to finish before I could get inside to check for my treasure.

My mouth flew open with the swinging of the door. The envelope was there and it looked full. I just glanced at it and did not stop to count it; for I knew that God had protected me once again.

I rushed out passing all those in line and praising God lifting my envelope to Him in praise. And I went out of that somber memorial declaring thanks and praise to God Almighty.

But the best of all was when I got back to our group on the bus. Everyone in our tour group, who had by now found out that I had lost something valuable, was waiting eagerly to hear my tragic news.

However, I had the wonderful opportunity and privilege to announce that God had answered my prayers. I shared that there was no other way to explain how my valuables had been protected.

With each statement that I was "lucky" I had the pleasure of sharing that luck had absolutely nothing to do with it. But instead it was the Hand of God. And that He had provided a shield of protection for me. And just as surely as Jesus had saved me from my sins, He had now saved my belongings. It was a glorious opportunity to share the Sovereignty of God.

I still pray that each and every person with my tour group that day may know Jesus as their Savior. And that He may be the Lord of their lives; that they may know the joy of trusting and praising my Great and Mighty God.

"Praise God from Whom all blessings flow. Praise Him all creatures here below. Praise Him above ye heavenly hosts. Praise Father, Son and Holy Ghost. Amen."

Blessings

*L*OOKING AT OUR BEDROOM furniture I thought once again how I wished we could buy something that I liked. We had been married for ten years and had only had hand-me-downs. It would be so nice to have something that I had picked out myself. But our budget was so tight; there was no way to shop for anything. So I thanked God for what I had and continued with being a homemaker and mother.

The fact that we were at another garage sale one morning soon thereafter was not unusual. Ever since Amanda had started to school, I had used the opportunity after dropping her off to go to all the garage sales in the area. The early morning venture often provided great treasures that fit our budget like a glove.

There were many people when we pulled up at the nice ladies house but she did have some fine items for sale. As I began to talk to her, all the other people seemed to dwindle down until finally it was just us. And then she asked me if I would be interested in any furniture. She had some things in the house she had planned to sell. But since she couldn't bring any of it out she offered to take me inside to see the items.

As we went in there was a chair and a dining set that were very nice but not what I needed. Then she remembered there was the guest bedroom suite she was going to sell as well. But, she apologized, it was an antique.

However, for me it was love at first sight. She did not have an amount calculated for it since she would need to check its worth. So I was sure it would be well out of my price range. Even yet my inward excitement was an explosion of eagerness at the mere possibility.

Back at home I checked my savings to see what we could afford to purchase the beautiful bedroom furniture. We only had six hundred dollars. Since there was the bed headboard and footboard, a beveled-edged mirrored dresser and a chest with a cedar-lined, lidded drawer plus a bonus matching straight chair with a beautiful tapestry cushioned seat, I thought there was no way we could afford it. I felt sure it would be well over a thousand dollars and there was just no way.

Therefore when she called to say the bedroom suite would probably be five hundred dollars, I told her I would take it! I was still in shock, and dancing, when she called back in a bit to say she was sorry.

I panicked thinking the deal was off. But instead she was calling to say she had forgotten the new mattress and box springs when she had figured the price. With the mattress set the total would be… six hundred dollars. The exact amount we had to spend! God is so good!

Then one day as I noticed something growing up next to the deck, it looked as if some kind of berries were hanging from the bush. Could that be blackberries?

It would not be the first time that God had given me fresh berries within reach. When we were first married and lived in an old rental house, I had thought about how I wished I could go pick strawberries like I had when I was growing up.

My Grandpa's brother had the next farm over where he grew strawberries every year. It seemed heavenly as a child to sit in the middle of a strawberry patch just picking and eating those fresh, juicy strawberries.

The next thing I knew I noticed what looked like strawberry plants growing in the flower bed next to the sidewalk. In no time at all the blooms had been replaced with berries. I would pick a cup or so every day of the biggest, sweetest strawberries I think I have ever eaten. God had truly supplied my every need.

Then a few years ago, as I watched people behind our new house across the field picking some of the largest, plumpest blackberries I have enjoyed, I wished so very much that I could go pick too. But my health did not allow me that opportunity.

I barely had enough strength to walk across the room. The heat and humidity would make it even worse. My arms and legs would begin to tremble and I would get so weak I would feel like I was going to pass out.

So all of my energy was needed for my job but I thanked God that He was providing those blackberries for someone. I knew that someday He would give me berries again. And He did much sooner than I had expected.

Soon thereafter, as I was driving down the driveway I noticed there were bushes growing beside the drive in the edge of the woods that looked strangely familiar. Pulling closer so that I could see them more clearly through the driver's window I realized that yes, those were blackberry bushes just covered with green berries.

How exciting! Thank you God! He had literally given me drive-thru blackberries!

I would normally have to get out of the car to pick my berries but there were times I could reach the berries through the car window. There had not been bushes there before and only God could have given me these wonderful, sweet treats.

And now there were bushes growing here at the edge of the deck. The limbs were hanging out over the deck where I could get fresh blackberries right outside my backdoor. And I must say again, "God is so good!"

> **"And my God will supply all your**
> **needs according to His riches in glory**
> **in Christ Jesus."** Philippians 4:19 NASB

God had definitely supplied my need that day they were working on our house. The contractor had told me that the huge pine tree next to our driveway would have to come down. If not it would be sure to fall soon and could destroy the house. I was hesitant but finally agreed.

I only had one request. There was a spindly, little dogwood tree growing against the pine tree. So I asked the contractor if he would try to save the dogwood when the pine tree was taken. He said I would need to talk to the power equipment operator. Only he would know if he could take the huge tree without hurting the tiny tree-ling.

The operator looked at me like I had a horn growing out of the center of my head. He said that since the trunk of the dogwood was against the pine, the roots would be intertwined. And because he was planning on pushing the pine tree over, he felt sure it would be impossible to save the dogwood.

I pleaded that he just try. I explained that if he would try to do the best he could, that I would be praying and would trust God to do the rest. So I headed for home with all the confidence that God would provide this pessimistic man with the reality of an Almighty, All-powerful God.

As I knelt to pray, I will admit that the roar of the equipment on the other side of the field was rumbling in my stomach. But I knew that God could give me this little piece of His creation.

When I drove back up the driveway a few hours later, the wide-eyed construction worker was pointing at the little dogwood tree and scratching his head. The pine tree was down. And of course the dogwood tree was still standing. I was not surprised. But he felt there was some need to try to explain the entire process.

He said that he had tried going in over the dogwood and pushing on the pine. He thought the dogwood would just be snatched up with the roots and the pressure of the pine.

But, he explained, as he began to push against the pine, the little, tiny dogwood had just stood strong. And when the pressure was so intense that the pine tree gave way and finally fell, the dogwood did not budge.

He admitted he had never seen anything like it. And he would never have believed it if he had not seen it for himself.

I explained that it was an answered prayer for that was exactly what I had asked for. Then he began mumbling about how somebody wanted that tree to stand, so it did.

"No, God wanted that tree to stand!"

And it has grown and thrived to this day…at the Hand of God.

"And all the trees will know that it is I, the Lord, who cuts the tall tree down and makes the short tree grow tall." Ezekiel 17:24 NLT

The dogwood tree God gave.

Rod's Prayer

ROD WAS HELPING IN the search for our dear friend Gary, who had been missing since the day before. So Rod had brought his boat to the lake to aide in the hunt. As he had looked out over the lake at the rescue effort with all those boats using sonar and dragging the lake, his heart had begun to break.

Gary had told him only a couple of weeks before that he had almost fallen out of the boat while out alone. Rod had asked if he had been wearing his life jacket at the time. When Gary said no, Rod told him he had better have it on all the time.

So why was he here now? How had this happened? Rod turned off the boat out in the middle of the lake, bowed his head and began to pray. Through tears and in agony he asked God to show him, to show him where to find Gary.

Looking back up to see how much the boat had drifted and to make sure he was not about to run ashore, he thought it had not drifted at all. Then he began to notice that although the wind was blowing, the water was splashing up against the sides of the boat which was not moving. He visually pinpointed his location by looking to each of the banks and for several minutes the boat stayed in the exact same spot.

He wanted to shout to the officials to check this site. He wanted to go over to them and bring them back to this particular spot. But who would believe a man who thought this was the right location just because the boat did not move?

So the search continued for three long, agonizing days and nights. On the day they found Gary, the spot where I had last seen them searching seemed the precise place where Rod later told me his boat had not moved. The very place that God had answered his prayer was where the search concluded. The exact place where God had showed him they could find our dear friend Gary.

> *"Trust in the Lord with all your heart and lean not on your own understanding. In all your ways acknowledge Him and He shall direct your paths."* Proverbs 3:5-6 NKJV

A Song in the Night

*I*AWOKE IN THE MIDDLE of the night with the song still playing through my head. I could hear the girl singing it and the melody was so clear and beautiful. I didn't know if I would be able to remember the song in the morning, so I started jotting down the words on a tablet on my nightstand.

But the next morning, the melody was still there. And all the words just seemed to be singing the desires of my heart.

What a wonderful gift God had given me. A song of my very own that I could sing to Him. I was so glad to be able to sing as I worked around the house or anytime I was alone with my Lord. It was a special blessing God had given…just for me.

And then during the sermon one Sunday morning, I felt that God wanted me to share my new gift. I felt He wanted me to share the testimony of how and why I felt God had given me the song. So that night I shared my story.

I had been working so hard at the church, at work and at home to please God but had felt that everything I had been doing was wrong. All I really wanted was to see the pleasure in God's eyes. You know like when you are playing the piano at your recital. And when you go to take your bow you look back at your parents to see if they are pleased with you.

Or like every time when you bat and get on base, you glance up at your parents to see if they are pleased with you. But most of all for me it was the look on my Grandpa's face in the hospital.

He had been very sick and had asked to see me. The problem was that at that time they didn't allow kids in the hospital rooms. So my father decided he would sneak me in. It was so much fun as Daddy spied out the best route and the most opportune time to go to Grandpa's room. He snuck me to the stairs and around corners like we were double-knot spies.

And then as I went into Grandpa's room, the look in his eyes when he saw me was stunning. He looked as if he was so very pleased to see me. As if all was made perfect at just seeing me. I could immediately see the pleasure in his eyes.

And now that is what I had been yearning for from God. That is what I wanted from my Heavenly Father. I so very much wanted to see the pleasure in His Eyes. And so one night He woke me up and gave me a song.

The song starts out about how I want to see that pleasure in my earthly father's eyes. And then moves on to how I want to see that pleasure in my Heavenly Father's Eyes.

Then I sang the song. Some people were shocked that I could even sing. Some were shocked that I had written a song. And still some people were just shocked that I had stood up and shared at all.

But the best thing about that day was I knew I had done what God had wanted me to do. And when I returned to my seat my husband whispered to me, "Well done thy good and faithful servant."

I didn't sing the song in public anymore. I didn't even tell my parents about any of it. I would still sing it sometimes when alone. And some people told me they enjoyed listening to the tape from that night. But other than that it remained a song for that one night, a song for me.

Until some seven years later, my father was dying from cancer. He had been in and out of the hospital for seven months and was now fighting his last day. The news was that the chemo was not working and that was his final option. There was no more hope and the nurse recommended we call in the family.

The odd thing was that when I stepped out into the hall to make some phone calls, the nurse came over to me. We had gone to church together years before and she had always been a special friend. She had been Daddy's nurse for months and now asked me if I had ever told Daddy about the song.

"What song?" I questioned.

"The song you sang at church," she explained, "the one that was partly about your father."

Since I had not told him about the song she suggested that I go ahead and share it with him. I was not thinking too clearly at the time but decided to follow her advice. I knew that they had said he may make it several days, but it might just be a matter of minutes.

So when I went back in, I bent over Daddy's bed and whispered in his ear the words to the song. I could not sing it because my Momma had told him that it was not "over until the fat lady sings". And since I knew I was somewhat fat, there was no way that I was going to sing! First, I whispered that in his ear and I am sure he was laughing on the inside.

When I was a child, I looked around me
To see the earth, the moon, the sun, the skies
I'd bring to you a single flower
Just to see the pleasure in your eyes.

If I could see the pleasure in your eyes,
If I could get a glimpse of your face shining bright
If I could only see, that you were pleased with me
If I could see the pleasure in your eyes.

And then as I grew I wandered wayward
But found out much to my surprise
That there was no joy greater
Than to see the pleasure in your eyes.

If I could see the pleasure in your eyes
If I could get a glimpse of your face shining bright
If I could only see, that you were pleased with me
If I could see the pleasure in your eyes.

So what can I bring You, Dear Jesus?
For the universe in Your Hands doth lie
I can bring You myself, a soul bound for hell
For that is all I have, that is all I can bring
For the mountains and valleys
Your Praises do sing,
I can give You myself, I can give You my life
Just to see the pleasure in Your Eyes.

If I can see the pleasure in Your Eyes
If I can get a glimpse of Your Face shining bright
If I can only see, that You are pleased with me
If I can see the pleasure in Your Eyes.

And now as I enter into Heaven
The book of my life You surmise.
You look o'er each page to see what I have done
And You find that my sins
have been covered by Your Son

For He paid the price, yes He gave His Life
So that I can see the pleasure in Your Eyes.

And now I see the pleasure in Your Eyes
And now I can see Your Face shining bright
And now I can see, that You are pleased with me
And I can see the pleasure in Your Eyes
For Jesus is the pleasure of Your Eyes
And I can see the pleasure in Your Eyes.

When I finished, a hospital chaplain had come into the room. When I glanced up and saw that it was a somewhat heavy woman, I whispered in Daddy's ear that he would never believe who was here. She asked if she could lead us in prayer. So we joined hands around my father's bed and had prayer for him. When she had said Amen, we all looked to my father.

He calmly took two quiet breathes...and was gone. It was a peaceful and precious moment I will never forget. I was so very thankful that God had allowed me to be with my father, holding his hand, when he left this earth. And I was so thankful God had placed the nurse there so I could share the song with him.

So he could hear the song...

before the fat lady sang.

This Gift

*A*s I DROVE PAST the church for what seemed like the hundredth time and in reality might have been, I thought one more time how nice it would be to work there. My friend worked there and the truth was I had always fought jealousy of her opportunity to work at the church. I often tried not to covet her job. I tried but admittedly it was one of those things I was continuously asking for forgiveness.

My father had been in the hospital again for cancer treatments. The first time he was there for thirty-one days, and the next was a couple of weeks, and another thirty-three days, and then back and forth for some seven months.

I had gone to see him every day he was there except for two days. I also kept working full-time. I worked in the national park some fifty minutes away from the hospital. And the church was only about five minutes from the hospital. So that only compounded my dream of working at the church.

My friend worked in accounting just as I did in my job then. And having served as the church treasurer and organist had only led me to feel the call to full-time service in God's Church. But her position was one of the few full-time positions that I felt that I was even somewhat qualified to do. So as I passed by that day I whispered a little prayer.

And then after seven months my father passed away. I wasn't traveling that route anymore. However working in the mountains gave me such a peace I could never have found anywhere else in the world. There is nothing to compare to the mountains in the morning, awakening to a fresh new day. And sitting by the river at lunch was a refreshing comfort that only God could have provided. He continually bathed me in His Presence. Just driving to and from work was a glorious time of praise to a Great and Mighty God.

And yet just three short months later, I received a phone call at work, a call that would change my life forever. My friend, Karen, who was the one working at the church I had been driving passed was on the other end. She wanted to know if I would be interested in working there at the church.

"Are you kidding? Of course I'm interested!" But what exactly was she talking about. She began to explain that the church's executive pastor was taking applications for a position to work as her assistant. I remember she asked if I would have a problem with having her as a boss.

"Of course not!" I just wanted to be, more than anything, where God wanted me. And if He was opening a door where I had already desired to be, there was no way I would turn down anything.

It turned out they were creating a new position. At the time I felt sure God was certainly leading them to create this position for me…just because I asked. God is so great and I cannot praise Him enough for how He has blessed me.

Karen needed a resume sent to her as quickly as possible. I rushed to update the one I had. And the next thing I knew, I was pulling into the parking lot for an interview. Although somewhat nervous, I found a certain peace in knowing that I was only there because this was confirming God's Will. There was one other great thing about the interview and that was the fact that I was allowed to share my testimony. Not only could I share it, but someone was actually enthused to hear it!

By the time I got back to work, there was a message on my machine to call her. Anxious, and stunned, I quickly called to find out it was to offer me the position. And although it would entail fewer responsibilities than I currently had, it would pay more money!

In a matter of days I was saying good-bye to a place I truly loved and was headed for a new opportunity to serve my Lord. And then after I had worked at the church only eleven months, Karen resigned. And I was offered her job! God is continually amazing me with His glorious gifts.

This person with almost no self-confidence was promoted to a director's position. And when I thought back over my life, I realized that all of the positions in the church where I had served had only been God training me for this calling, for His calling. Even my previous working experience had been His preparation for me.

For one thing, I had been hired because I had previous experience with the accounting software the church was using. But soon after I started, new accounting software was purchased. Of course, I had also had experience with setting up six different accounting softwares in my previous employments so that was not a problem.

And since then there have been numerous other new softwares added to the financial system. But none of these were as difficult as my past experiences. And my having worked as a payroll clerk prepared me for many of the payroll issues. Having worked as the treasurer helped to prepare me to do the pastors' nonstandard payroll. And of course having worked with children had helped me to learn to always expect the unexpected!

I had served on the counting committee to prepare the deposits. I had served on other committees, taught classes, played the piano and organ and sung in the choir. I had even written play scripts, made props and scenery and acted in dramas. The church where I now worked had grown largely as a result of their professional-like production of the Living Christmas Tree. All of my experiences have helped to give insight into each of the ministries within the church.

I know now that God had been preparing me for my entire life to work in His Church. I know that He had called me to serve Him in my position. And I know that in October some eight years ago, God gave me…

this gift.

"For I know the plans I have for you," declares the Lord, *"plans to prosper you and not to harm you, to give you hope and a future."* Jeremiah 29:11 NIV

The Father

WHEN MY DADDY WAS in the hospital for his last Father's Day, I asked him what I could give him or what I could do for him for his special day. After disagreeing that he did not want or need anything, he finally consented. "Just make me a card," he said.

So I sat down, like a little forty-four year old child and typed out, printed up, cut and pasted the following inside of his last hand-made, with love Father's Day card.

Happy Father's Day to the World's Greatest Dad!

*You always taught me from the day I was born
all the things I needed to know for life.*

*You taught me to be curious, to seek
knowledge and to learn.*

*You taught me to love the beauty, majesty
and wonder of what God created.*

*You taught me to learn from others (especially from
people like you who have tried and tested and know).*

You taught me to be honest, trustworthy and fair.

You taught me to sing for joy.

You taught me to laugh, and laugh, and laugh.

And yes, "laughter is good medicine".

*Above all, Daddy, you taught me more
than you will ever know of the love of The
Father and what His Word means.*

*I love and adore you and hope that this day is
the first day of another great year for...*

The World's Greatest Dad!

Daddy cried when he read it. I really didn't mean to make him cry. I wanted to take it all back. But still I did want him to know how very much I loved him.

And although I never explained to him how he had taught me about The Father and His Word, I think he somehow knew. He knew that God expects us to love Him and only Him. And He expects us to trust Him and to depend on Him and only Him. He expects us to talk to Him and spend time with Him. That is why Jesus has told us to "Love the Lord your God with all your heart, with all your soul and with all your mind" in Matthew 22:37 NKJV.

Then I forgot about the card until...he died. We were planning his funeral just a little over a month after giving him the card. And I was feeling overwhelmed with wanting to prove to the world that he really was a good father. So I gave a copy to Rod of both the card and the words to the song God had granted me. And Rod, in turn, gave them to the pastor to read at the funeral.

It somehow comforted my guilt over his death. And was the only good thing I remember about his funeral.

"Grace, mercy, and peace will be with you from God the Father and from the Lord Jesus Christ, the Son of the Father, in truth and love." 2 John 1:3 NKJV

"The Lord gave, and the Lord has taken away; Blessed be the name of the Lord." Job 1:21 NKJV

Like a Son

WHEN MY OLDEST DAUGHTER was five, a visiting preacher, and friend, at our church preached a powerful message to mothers. The message was about raising your children and how important it is to pray for them. At one point he looked straight at me and asked me by name if I was praying for my girls. Of course, I shook my head yes.

But he went on with a list of things to be praying for your children. Was I praying for their school, for their teachers, for their friends, for their future? Their future would be the college they would choose or not choose; their career choice; and most importantly their spouse. He emphasized we pray for their future spouse and not to wait until they were married.

I began praying that day. I prayed for each of my girls specifically. I prayed just as he had suggested for their teachers and what friends they would have. I prayed for the lives of those friends and the influence they would have on each other. Their education and career choices were included too.

But the one thing I prayed for the most was who they would date. And eventually who they would marry. I would pray for these young men, boys at the time, just as I prayed for my own daughters. I prayed for their salvation before they ever started dating my daughters. I prayed for their education, teachers, friends and family.

One specific prayer, for these family members I would not meet for possibly decades, was that when I met him I would not feel the need to get to know him. That he would seem familiar. That I would feel as if I had known him for years.

I prayed also that when I met him I would love him instantly, like the first time you see your own baby. That I wouldn't love him like a son-in-law but would love him like a son.

There were times when I would feel like there was some specific reason I needed to pray for him. On one instance I felt sure there was a problem with his family. I prayed for all of them. I prayed especially for his parents to know how to handle whatever was wrong. I even felt Amanda's future husband was the middle of three boys.

Then as Amanda began dating, I would pray for these young men she dated. But none of them seemed like what I had asked for. They were all nice boys and I loved them all. And I knew that she would be the one to decide who she married, but still.

Eventually she became upset about some of her friends getting married and she couldn't find her own special someone. And she had asked me when she was going to find that person to be her lifelong friend. I just told her that she needed to be patient.

But she questioned on where she could possibly meet someone now since she was out of college and working at a preschool. The only men she ever saw were fathers coming to pick up their children. I explained that there might be some child's uncle or much older brother but she disagreed about that possibility. Or she may meet this someone at the mall or at the movies or at some restaurant. Or he may be a friend of a friend. For all she knew, she might meet someone at the ball field. She disagreed since she played on an all-girls team. But I assured her that someone just might know someone or…who knows?

As always, I talked to God about it and trusted that He would lead in His time. And soon He did.

She came home and said her coach had wanted to know if she could give Amanda's name and number to her nephew. It seemed rather odd at the time but as it turned out my in-laws had already met him years earlier. The next thing I knew, they were dating and my daughter was stopping by our house with him to get something out of her old bedroom.

The very minute I started talking to this new young man in her life, he seemed so very familiar. It was as if I had known him all my life. Some of his actions and mannerisms reminded me of my cousins. And some things reminded me of dear friends. And some things even reminded me of my dad.

And his sense of humor, although unusual, seemed to fit our family perfectly. But better yet, it practically mirrored Amanda's! And he was so polite and genteel, that I just loved him from the moment I met him.

It was so much like the first time I saw my own children. From that minute and beyond I considered him one of my kids.

Some ten months later, they were married. Thank You God for answered prayer!

One down and one to go!

Uganda?

As Rod leaned over me before church began, he poked Jennifer on the other side of me. He asked her if she and her new boy friend were getting serious. She just shrugged her shoulders with a somewhat smirky grin. And then he asked if she thought they were getting married. I just pushed him back over to his end of the pew and whispered, "Good grief! They've only been dating a couple of weeks."

Everyone by now was used to her father's ridiculous questions that were always at the strangest of times. But I was still rolling my eyes and shaking my head as she wrote out a note to him on the back of the bulletin.

I had to read it before passing it on. And once he read it I had to snatch it from him to keep and treasure forever.

The note said: *I don't waste time with someone I cannot see myself marrying or is hindering my walk with God. So I am not giving my heart to this kid until God allows me to 'cause He is the one holding it. So until then I can leave at any time or proceed if He wills.*

I penned at the bottom of the note, *I am so proud of you!* Actually I had to wonder if my pride in my daughter was being sinful. She had just returned from a three week trip to Uganda, Africa.

When she had first told me about the trip, I had to ask exactly where Uganda was. She had obviously done her research because she told me in detail about the culture and the economy and the enormous orphan rate. But her reason for picking Uganda was what had impressed me most.

She had been to a Christian conference where she felt she could not sing a particular song about her commitment to God because she did not feel like it was true. She prayed at that time for God to lead her to that place He would have her to go. After that God seemed to be directing her to Uganda. And like me she thought, "Where in the world is Uganda?"

She had learned that there was an orphanage in Kampala, Uganda in east Africa that needed mission's volunteers to work for any length of time. Her major was in Early Childhood Development so she knew this was part of God's plan. And the orphanage even had a guest house she could stay in. Plus it was in the city where the major airport was located.

At my insistence, after all she was only twenty and to a mother always my baby, she asked her friends, Erika and Nate, to go with her. And since they were newlyweds eager to do missions work with orphans, they agreed enthusiastically.

She immediately fell in love with the children of Uganda. And Erika and Nate fell in love with one certain little boy so much that they decided to adopt him!

But one of the greatest things about the trip was that on her first Sunday there, when they got to the church, the first song they sang was the exact song she had felt she could not sing at the conference just a few months earlier. The very reason she had began this mission from the other side of the world. So God had confirmed that she was where He wanted her. And she was doing exactly what He wanted her to do. She could sing the song now!

Then Erika asked her to go back to Uganda with her to adopt their baby boy. But it would be in March when Jennifer was supposed to be in school. However, after praying about the trip and checking at school about her classes, she learned that the classes she needed to graduate would not be offered until summer. God had confirmed that He wanted her to go back to Uganda. They would be able to work and stay at the orphanage again while proceeding with the process for the adoption.

So for ten weeks they worked on the adoption and cared for the babies at the orphanage. And during that time they were able to take some of the babies to the doctor to get some much needed medical attention. Lives of precious babies were saved because they were there. However, disheartened through many ordeals with the court system without a final hearing they were on their way back to the airport to leave for the states. Suddenly Erika's phone rang to say a hearing was scheduled! Jennifer was able to continue the trip home while Erika was able to stay.

Erika and Nate were eventually able to have their little son home with them and the adoption was finalized. And even now Jennifer continues to hope to go back to Uganda someday. She still feels called to minister to and care for these precious babies, these precious children of God.

And God is using her missions work to bless me…and many others as well.

> *"I thank my God upon every remembrance of you."* Philippians 1:3 NKJV

Eight Babies

O NE NIGHT I HAD a very strange dream. In the dream I was walking through a dark, shadowy mist and leading a group of people. I could see my friend Janet at the front of the group. She was followed by Ramona and Betty and beyond that I could not clearly make out the faces of the rest of the group.

But I could see the shadowy images of these sad, suffering people. As I turned to lead them to their children, I noticed there was something encircling my chest, a sack of sorts with eight pockets or pouches for carrying these tiny babies. Eight babies I carried close to my heart.

When I awoke, I tried to make some sort of sense out of the eerily, serene dream. It was both heart breaking and comforting at the same time.

As I thought back I knew Janet, Ramona and Betty had each lost a grown child recently, all in their twenties and all sudden tragic losses. But why would I be carrying eight babies around my heart.

Could these be the babies of the parents who had lost a child? I began to ponder the possibility that I had known eight families who had gone through this agonizing, gut-wrenching ordeal. And I had three already. Names of those I had known who had lost a child began flooding in but it seemed there were so many more than eight.

So I started off counting those who I had talked to about their child's death, tried to comfort or console in some way. First was Becky who I had worked with for a short time when her son at nineteen had died in a car wreck. She had been devastated. And I can still see her face and hear her voice as she had shared her struggles in dealing with her grief. I still pray for her even though that was over twenty years ago and I never see her anymore.

Then second was my daughter, Jennifer's teacher at school. Mrs. Quillen had lost her son, Ben, that school year when she had gone in to wake him up. At just seventeen years of age, he had died in his sleep. In a newspaper article his father had said he felt that his son had died of a broken heart over the lost condition of some of his friends. My heart and Jennifer's had broken for Mrs. Quillen.

She had told me how comforting Jennifer had been to her. She would be crying and would look over and see Jennifer was crying too. Or Jennifer would come and just give her a hug. I still pray for Mrs. Quillen.

And thirdly there was Thresea, my sister-in-law's son, Josh. He was one of those stunning young men you could not help but love. But tragically he had been driving home one morning after working the night shift when his car had ran off the road.

When we had walked into the emergency room, Thresea grabbed me and said, "Please pray!" I know she meant to pray for her son and I had already been praying, but she is the one who continues to need the prayer. So I have been praying for her specifically ever since.

Fourth was Jennifer's friend, Emily. She was a bubbly, blonde who was full of life and having fun. My older daughter, Amanda, had gone to school with Emily's sister, Kayla, since kindergarten. So Jennifer and Emily had been seeing each other at school, girl scouts and ballgames since they were infants, eleven short years.

Emily had been in a car accident. Her mother, Sandra, told me she got to spend some time alone with Emily before they turned off the machines. My heart still breaks for Sandra and I continue to pray for her and Kayla as well.

Thinking of all of these tragic losses is so heart breaking. I mourn for these people and yet, life goes on. They have had to pick up and move on. But the hurt never goes away. And no one really ever gets over the loss of a child.

And still yet the fifth seems the most heartbreaking of all. I can just not come up with any good reason why God would allow a mere child, a toddler, to die. But yet I know in His infinite wisdom only He knows the real impact and blessings that have come from the life and death of Lance Evan Russell.

He was and continues to be the most handsome three year old I have ever seen. I can say that with all confidence because no child has ever caught my eye the way that he did. I was not his teacher in class nor did I have any real interaction with him, but I always noticed him. Always coming in or going out of church with his parents or grandparents, he had a striking personality.

He was only three when he was diagnosed with Acute Myelogenous Leukemia. His courageous battle was only ten months. But his parents' documentation of his journey, his battle, was monumental in my respect and admiration for him.

His parents, Ed and Tiffany, had to watch their only son as this horrible cancer destroyed his life. I thank God for the witness Ed and Tiffany have shown through this nightmare. They have truly shown us He was with them through the storm.

Ed continued Lance's website for years. His stories about Lance were wonderful. And his articles about God's Word were so insightful and inspiring. And Tiffany's testimony by singing in the choir after their loss was such a great witness of a God who is Worthy to be praised. I aspire to be more like her.

I pray they may know what a blessing they have been to me and many others. I pray for them constantly.

Then there was the horrible news I got at work just some eight years ago. LeeAnn, the daughter of our organist, had been found and had obviously died in her sleep. She had suffered from an extremely painful disease all of her life.

But that was not what had struck me when I had first been in a class with LeeAnn just months earlier. She was a vibrant, outgoing, bubbly young lady. She had spoken with a much greater wisdom about God than most any young person her age. And she had a passion for the elderly, because as she explained, she could really relate to a lot of the complications they were facing. As I had later observed, they truly loved and adored her too.

Betty, her mother, amazed me by continuing to play the organ through what I am sure were some of the hardest days of her life. She played on, or should I say praised, even through times of tears.

God led me to pray for Betty on many different occasions when I felt she was just having a hard day. And I still pray for her whenever I hear the song "In the Garden". It was one of LeeAnn's favorite songs that Betty played on the piano at LeeAnn's funeral. So LeeAnn must be the sixth baby.

But more tragedy was yet to come. In November of 2008, I got word that a dear friend from work had fallen while hiking in the mountains. Jeremy, just twenty-six, had been hiking with friends to a waterfall when he had slipped above the falls.

His landing on the rocks below had caused such extensive injuries that he could not recover. Since I worked with his mother also, my heart broke for both of them. I truly loved Jeremy, almost like a son.

How could this have happened? Just a couple of months before, I had sat Jeremy down and talked to him about hiking alone. I had warned him at length about hiking above the falls. I had cautioned him to never ever go up there even if he was with friends and they were going.

We had talked on more than one occasion about the dangers of hiking in the mountains. I knew! I had worked inside the national park and had heard story after story of just such incidences.

I even stressed that I was warning him with all the urgency that I would have for my own children. And I explained that I knew that he was a boy and studies had shown that boys at that age do not think through the possibilities. They just do not see what is at risk because of some of the chemicals in their brains. It's almost like a shortage in the electrical wiring.

I told him to decide in his mind right now how he would handle that situation. Decide right now to not follow anyone into that dangerous situation. So why had he?

When I had to pull out his file to get his life insurance beneficiary, cold chills ran over my already sickened body. The memories of the day he had turned it in and our conversation came rushing in and flooding my mind like a raging river.

He had turned it in and insisted on explaining his beneficiary although I told him that who he wanted to list as the beneficiary was really none of my business. He sat down, and now looking back, it was as if he was planning what he knew was inevitable. It had been four years since we'd had that conversation, but with that same piece of paper in my hand, it seemed like yesterday.

At the time I thought the conversation was very strange for someone so young to have put so much thought into his beneficiary on his life insurance policy. Surely it would be fifty years before anyone would ever care about Jeremy's life insurance. But then, there I was, holding the form in my trembling hand. And I knew that God had allowed Jeremy the insight into his own future.

Somehow Jeremy had known. Somehow God had given him the foresight about his soon approaching death. And somehow the very warning I had given to Jeremy about what could happen in the mountains had been exactly what had happened. or maybe it was not intended by God as a warning, but instead as preparation for

Jeremy for what was to come. And everyone who knew him would agree that there was nowhere in the world that Jeremy would have rather spent his last day walking on this earth.

And yet through much heart break and many tears, Ramona and Dwayne continue to be an inspiration to me. They continue to lift their voices and their hands in praise to a Great and Mighty God. Ramona's witness through this entire tragedy and beyond has been a constant reminder of the Grace of God.

I have to pray for Jeremy's family constantly for I know too that an awesome, young man, a light in this world, has gone out. A light has gone out...out of this world...and to another world to be with the Light of the world.

> *"Then Jesus again spoke to them saying, "I am the Light of the world; he who follows Me will not walk in the darkness, but will have the Light of life."* John 8:12 NASB

And now I realize too that while Jeremy is the seventh baby, then that would make Gary the eighth baby. Gary whose mother, Janet, was now closest following me in my dream is the eighth baby I carry close to my heart.

Janet and I had met for lunch while Jeremy was still in the hospital. She had talked to me extensively about how she just did not think she could cope with the loss of her son, her only son.

And then in April she got the call. Gary was missing from his boat at the lake. My first thoughts were that this is her nightmare. Her most dreaded fears had come true.

But the nightmare had just started. It was three long, tortuous days and nights before Gary was found. Another couple of days for the autopsy and then the funeral was one week later.

And then the nightmare continued as a precious momma and daddy were home alone without their only child. The very child they had adored and prayed over for more than the twenty-two years of his life.

How can you console parents who have lost their everything? How do you explain why? Why him?

The only explanation I could find was that his life and death could be used to reach so very many people for Jesus Christ that could not be reached by any other way. These people need to be reached and soon for Jesus is coming!

Ed and Janet have grasped out of desperation the fact that they will not see their son again until they reach Heaven themselves. And yet they have held strong to God and His Promises. As they continue to see what a great impact Gary had on the people who knew him, they use every possible opportunity to reach those people for Jesus Christ. Janet has written letters to many of his friends. And has even written a book entitled "Peering Through A Mist, A Mom's Journey in Loss and God's Grace" which has already touched many lives.

In addition, since his death, numerous individuals have come to know Jesus as their Savior and Lord. One person actually accepted Christ at Gary's funeral!

> *"Greater love hath no man than this,*
> *that a man lay down his life for*
> *his friends."* John 15:13 KJV

And, yes, Jesus is coming!

There were many more people I knew who had lost a child. But there were none that I could say that I had been there for them. There were none that I had actually tried to comfort or console.

I have considered my dream and realized that I actually have been trying to help all of these people through this dark, shadowy mist we call life. Trying to help them through, to the Heaven where their children now abide. And I realized that I do in fact now carry these eight precious babies,

close to my heart.

"Blessed are those who mourn, For they shall be comforted." Matthew 5:4 NKJV

The Saddest Obituary

Reading over the obituary of my husband's old family friend, my eyes kept searching frantically for the answer. I desperately needed the answer to my questions and prayers of over fifteen years now. Holding and looking at the newspaper, my thoughts raced back to the saddest Bible I had ever seen.

A friend I had been inviting to come to church for months had finally came. From the choir I noticed her in the back row of the sparsely filled church auditorium. As I eagerly waited for the choir director to dismiss the choir, I scratched a note and slipped it to Rod. I told him I would be going to the back to sit with my friend instead of sitting in our usual spot.

Then anxiously making my way to the back row of the church, I slipped in next to her and welcomed her to the service. As she moved her Bible to make room for me to sit, I grinned to myself at the brand-new, bright, shiny white Bible she carefully laid on her lap. I was so excited to see her enthusiasm at coming to worship our Lord. Just thinking that she had gone to buy a new, white Bible so much like my old one, was positively moving.

My thoughts wandered to the countless hours I had spent absorbing the priceless wisdom held within my now tattered and more-like cream colored Bible. The love I felt for this old book was beyond a mere affection. But looking at it on my lap compared to the one on her lap was at that moment somewhat embarrassing.

It looked as if I had not taken very good care of it. And although I had never really run over it with the car, no one could actually verify that by its appearance. So I carefully crammed it under my purse on my other side hoping she did not notice. Maybe I could get it out when the pastor started without her seeing the cover.

Then as he began with the scripture reference, I reached for my Bible, carefully using the bulletin to block her view. Turning back with my Bible opened to the correct book and chapter, I slyly moved the bulletin from obstructing her view and slid it underneath. She was still searching for the scripture and had not noticed. I breathed a sigh of relief and settled myself to focus on the message.

But tears began to fill my eyes as I looked back down at my page to read along with the pastor. Glancing over at her Bible to see that she had found the correct reference, I noticed the pages. The edges of the pages were extremely yellowed with age. This Bible was not new at all. It had been sitting on some shelf gathering dust for what appeared to be years. And now, the worn out Bible on my lap was by all means the more beautiful of the two. And the old, unused, bright, shiny, white Bible, I had minutes ago thought was so nice, was now the saddest Bible I had ever seen.

How could anyone own a Bible and not be captivated by the love of God throughout His Word? So now I am remembering that question as I am skimming over what turned out to be the longest obituary I have ever seen.

First there was the list of family members who were deceased. That was followed by the list of each and every surviving family member, spouse, children, children-in-law and grandchildren.

This was followed up by his military career, which included battles he had fought and medals he had earned. Plus the account of his and his sons ventures back to Europe to visit those places where he had served.

His career was included. And organizations in which he had been involved. All followed by the arrangements for the funeral.

But my head dropped and all hope diminished as I realized there was no church. I feverishly raced back over the wording to verify, no church at all. There was no church and no pastor which led me to believe that there was no relationship with my wonderful Savior. No relationship...and no hope.

Numerous men I knew had visited this man over the years in order to try to lead him to know Jesus Christ. Even Rod had gone and talked to him about his spiritual condition. The old soldier had cried as they talked but had not accepted Jesus. And as far as I knew, he had never turned to the One who had fought the ultimate battle for him. The One who had truly given His Life for our eternal freedom, for our eternal home in Heaven.

As the Sacrifice was realized, without any known acceptance of His Gift, my tears were wetting the pages of the paper. Not for the death of this man, but for his loss of life, eternal life. And for his loss of Love. This was without a doubt the saddest obituary I had ever read.

Jesus said to him, "I am the way, the truth, and the life. No one comes to the Father except through Me." John 14:6 NKJV

A Bird in the House

"**G**LENDA, WHY IS THERE a bird in the house?" Rod yelled from the living room. I had not even heard him come in but could he be talking about the bird figurine I had just bought at my favorite boutique? I thought for sure I had put it in the bathroom and he sounded like he was in the living room.

"What are you talking about?" I inquired as I rushed back to the living room. He stood staring and pointing in disbelief up at the cathedral window. Sure enough, fluttering around trying to find her way out was a bird, a wren I think.

I squealed with delight as she flew across the eighteen foot ceiling to the front window to seek her freedom. She fluttered around there, then back across to the back window. And back and forth she flew as I screamed for joy at the sheer excitement. I was trying to follow her every move and frantically trying to think how we could ever catch or help this poor, little bird.

As Rod was running around trying to open as many doors and windows as possible, I suddenly remembered the net. It was supposed to be a child's butterfly net but I had bought it to catch small things out of the pool. I came running, sure that we could "catch and release" her now.

But I felt pretty silly as I looked at the two foot or so handle for the net in my hand. Considering the eighteen foot ceilings at best I could only reach about seven or eight feet. However, I was still sure we could help this poor bird. As she continued to fly back and forth, I screamed every time she made a pass over the ceiling fan.

And then she flew right past the open door of freedom instead to the parlor. She tried to escape through the bay windows and then landed on top of the floor lamp.

I've got her now! I hurried to the parlor and was chasing her around with the net when I finally got her. But as I moved the net to try to get her outside, she escaped. She started flying circles around my head.

All I could remember was the movie Alfred Hitchcock had made about the birds. And that woman being attacked by those birds pecking her head was suddenly me, even though there was no actual pecking.

I screamed, and jumped, and swatted, and fluttered myself. The bird flew a couple of circles around me and then did the strangest thing.

She landed on my shoulder. She landed on the very shoulder that had been trying to catch her in the net. She just sat there as calmly and serenely as a peaceful summer's night.

She was at total peace. But I on the other hand had an all-out panic attack. I screamed and flailed until I knocked her to the floor. Since she was a little stunned from the smack of my hand and then the impact of the floor, I managed to scoop her in the net and headed for the front door.

But my nervousness and my husband's help just aided her escape. She flew to the nearest tree, one of those fake ficus trees that seemed to make a perfect perch for her. And the tree was an amiable place for me to try netting her again. As I awkwardly missed once more, she flew across the room yet again just passing the opened back door to freedom.

She landed in another one of those trees and looked most content to remain there, not at all troubled that I was speedily in pursuit. I clumsily dropped her from the net, or maybe I knocked her with the net, onto the rug in front of the opened door.

She just sat looking back at me as if to say, "Do you really want me to go? Do I really have to go out there?"

As I took the net and nudged her little hopping body to freedom, I had to wonder why this bird did not want to leave. Half hopping and half flying over the threshold, she landed and looked back at me one last time.

Why was I making her go? She flew over to the edge of the pool and just sat there. As if contemplating her next move while reviewing the moments we had shared.

She still remained perfectly calm. She sat there for quite some time as I stressed over having ran out one of God's precious creatures. And then as if to say her mission was complete, she flew away.

My heart sank at the departure of my new found friend. It was that happy-sad feeling. Happy for her, that she had finally found her way home. But sad for me, that there was a new empty in my house.

However now that she was gone, I was filled with an overwhelming peace. She had helped me to see what a short time we have here in this home. How there are times of joy and excitement. And other times of bumping into things we did not even see or realize were there.

And in the midst of what seems to be the most tumultuous of all, we can rest our all on His Shoulders, for He is the Comforter. He can give us perfect peace,

the peace that passes all understanding.

"Be anxious for nothing,…

but in everything by prayer and supplication, with thanksgiving, let your request be made known to God; and the peace of God, which surpasses all understanding, will guard your hearts and minds through Christ Jesus." Philippians 4:6-7 NKJV

The Lake

As I approached the lake and saw the huge crowd of people on the shore, boats in the water and a parking lot full of empty boat trailers, the tears began to flow. They flowed with all the intensity of the waterfalls in the mountains. The tears were as determined as the winding river flowing down the mountainside. I could not hold them back. I could not deter them. I just had to let them come. And come they did.

As I walked along the water's edge, peering out at the slew of boats and fishermen awaiting the start of the 3rd Annual Gary Lindsey Memorial Fishing Tournament, my heart was heavy. My vision was blurred. I love this lake...and I hate this lake.

It had given so much to me in my lifetime. And it had taken so much. The lake had taken more than I would have ever anticipated or dreamed possible when I used to come with my family for one of our great boating adventures.

It had all started when I was just a child in elementary school and Daddy had bought a boat. Not a big boat but a small runabout. Made for riding or maybe skiing and Daddy thought for fishing too if we wanted. It was light blue on the top and white on the bottom. The seats and carpet were blue and although it was used, it held within it a limitless number of hours of pure pleasure for me.

Daddy would get the boat ready and off to the lake we would be in a matter of minutes. We would go up the river and spend the day just drifting back down. Or we would ride the lake for countless hours. Or we would find a nice cove to do some fishing. And when the fish stopped biting, we would just jump in for a cool swim.

Momma would always bring along a small cooler with sandwiches and drinks or Daddy's favorite, sardines. Somehow they tasted pretty good on the lake with a cracker or two.

A few times we had loaded the tents and sleeping bags under the hull and gone up on Norris Lake to camp in the wilderness near where my mother had grown up. She had walked there with her father to go fishing when she was a little girl. For me as a child, it was a thrilling adventure.

Many times we had taken our boat to my father's sister's houseboat up on Cherokee Lake to spend the weekend. I loved to fish from the side of the houseboat. I loved being on the water.

Sleeping and eating on the water seemed so perfect to me. I loved swimming too. One time when we got there I kept pestering Daddy to go swimming. So he just picked me up and threw me in, clothes and all! I thought it was so much fun I was laughing underwater. It still makes me laugh to think of it.

Then there was the cabin up on another part of Norris Lake owned by the company where my father worked. Daddy managed the calendar for employees to schedule vacations there. It was on an island of sorts. They had built up the road to get to it and had it gated for security.

The cabin seemed huge. It had two bedrooms and a loft with about eight beds. Since Daddy kept the calendar he would know if anyone cancelled at the last minute or was arriving late. And he knew when the cabin was just empty between visitors. He would just come home and tell us to get our stuff together, we were going for the night or weekend.

I loved the cabin because it had a dock and a little row boat that Daddy would let me take out by myself. I could paddle around the cove first thing in the morning and fish. It was great! I would spend all the time I could fishing or swimming. Sometimes I think I would just live in the water, if I could.

I have told people that I have always been happy wherever I am as long as there is water. I love the water. I love the lake.

But as I keep getting closer to the dam, the memories were rushing in. Memories were overflowing me just as the waters released by the dam. All those times we had to come to just take the boat through the lock were vivid recollections. It had truly taught me of the enormous responsibility of the engineers, construction workers and now the dam's operators. This enormous dam which controlled the mighty rivers to create the wondrous, peaceful waters of the lake was a cold, concrete memory of the past.

This was the same dam that Daddy drove me over almost every day we were on our way to work. I loved riding with him to work because it gave us, just me and Daddy, a chance to talk like we had never had all my life.

And crossing the lake here had always brought back those great memories. Not just memories of boating and skiing but even more. Memories of taking my girls to the sandy beach park next to the dam where they could play in the cool, refreshing waters of the lake.

Nevertheless crossing here had become a horrible, dreaded memory. The son of a friend of Rod's had met with a horrible accident here that had taken his life.

Levi was just seventeen when he had come with two friends below the dam to fish. He had fished here before and was following his father's careful instructions of not getting too close to the waters when the turbines were running.

He knew how strong their draw was and how powerful the pull. But one of his friends did not understand. He slipped and fell into the waters. Not being a good swimmer and being pulled toward the turbines of the dam, Levi jumped in to save his friend. He reached his friend but could not pull him to safety.

So with a mighty shove he pushed his friend toward the shore. His friend was able to reach the ground of safety. But the push had sent Levi out deeper into the suction of the turbine driven waters.

He had fought with all his might swimming the churning waters for some twenty minutes before he was finally pulled under. Rescue squad members and the dam's employees had turned off the turbines and used every possible means to reach him, to rescue him. But to no avail. He was gone from sight and it would be some time before he was finally recovered. I hate the lake.

And again, *"Greater love hath no man than this, that a man lay down his life for his friends."* John 15:13 KJV

The crowd is overwhelming. The number of trucks with boat trailers is smothering me. I don't think I can breathe. My heart is pounding.

As I get closer I start to cry, trying to fight back the tears I finally give in to their exhaustive tremendous hold on me. It is Gary's memorial tournament, a fishing tournament to honor the memory of my dear friends' twenty-two year old son.

A young man who I was honored to count as a friend myself as was all who knew him. And an avid fisherman who loved the lake possibly more than I had loved it myself.

A good swimmer who had just over two years ago for some unknown reason fell out of his fishing boat into the icy, cold waters of the lake he so loved. And although he had been reported missing almost immediately, he was not found for three days. Three days of gut-wrenching agony, three days of denial, three days of one thread of hope.

On the second day of the search, I could not stand just standing anymore. Fishermen were out in their boats searching the banks while the rescue agencies ran sonar, dived and used every means possible to find Gary. Countless volunteers searched the banks and wooded areas around where his boat had gone out of control and landed on the shore.

There were numerous more of us who just sat and prayed and paced and prayed. I remember looking at the lake once and thinking how eerily peaceful it looked, eerie and peaceful at the same time. I remember thinking that was so strange. Never once in my entire life had I seen any lake as eerie. That was not until then.

Crossing back over the bridge to the other side of the lake, I parked and walked down to the water's edge. I knelt down there and while holding one hand in the water I began to pray.

I prayed that God would deliver Gary, alive and well to the shores of this lake. I prayed that He would have the lake spit him out as the great fish spat out Jonah on the shore. I prayed that he would be found and rushed to the hospital to find that he only had minor injuries that no one could explain…except for the Hand of God.

I prayed that his delivery could only be justified as an act of God and that through that act many would come to know Jesus Christ and He would be glorified. I begged and pleaded with God and tears poured down my cheeks…just as they did now.

Then I prayed, if it was not according to God's will to deliver Gary alive, for God to deliver his body back to his parents. I prayed that he would be found, not on the muddy, murky bottom of the lake. And not on the top of the lake, floating, where that image would be forever imbedded in the minds of all those who found him, forever haunting them.

But I prayed that Gary would be found floating between the water's surface and bottom of the lake. I prayed that it would be as if he were just drifting along. I prayed that when his body was recovered it would be astonishing to all those who found him at how good he looked.

I prayed that to his mother and father he would look so peaceful as if he were asleep. I prayed that his coloring would be normal and not pale and washed out from being in the water.

My hand still in the cold, cold water, I asked God to give this child who was touching this water back to his mother and father so that they could tell him good-bye. I prayed that this nightmare would not go on one second longer than was necessary and that all could withstand and trust God's timing.

I started making my way around the cove and wandered up into the wooded area, just looking and calling out to Gary. Then I came upon a lush, grassy area that looked like someone had been lying down.

"Gary," I called, "is this where you were? Gary! Gary! Where are you?" *Or is this where God has laid you to rest until He was ready to return you to your family?*

Just beyond the grassy area was a large assembly of daffodils blooming brilliantly in the spring sunshine. In this remote area, on this dismal day, they were a strangely beautiful sight; a reminder that God is God, the Great Creator.

No house in sight but yet there were three varieties of daffodils. I thought they were there just for me and to take to Janet, so I picked them all.

As I started back across the bridge, I realized the flowers were not all for Janet. But the flowers were so I would have something to offer; something for Janet, Gary's mother…and something for Gary.

So I stopped the car and walked back across the bridge to the point which was most centered over the waters. There I took some of the flowers and dropped them into the waters of the lake below as I continued to pray for Gary's rescue. I praised God for His comfort, for His supplying my need.

And then I proceeded on to take the flowers to Janet. I tried to explain how I had found the flowers. But before I could say anything, she screamed out, "Oh, my favorite flowers!" I think since she was still in shock she did not realize that there were no more of these flowers blooming anywhere in the county, not one to be found anywhere, except here.

And I had found these flowers as if planted there. By whom I don't know, but for whom I know with all my heart. These flowers were kept there for me to find for Janet. Had God put them there? I do not know, but I do know He grew them. And He led me to them.

I do also know that He knew all along that they were Janet's favorite flowers. And I know that He knew I needed a clear sign that He heard my prayers and was right there with Gary. And He would be right there with all of us through this and every storm of our lives.

Soon after I delivered the flowers to Janet there was a tornado warning so the search was postponed and we were evacuated. We prayed that the winds would not damage the area or disturb the search. And, just as we had asked, God caused the storm to go totally around the sight with not a bit of storm in that immediate area around the search site. God had protected us in this one storm of life from this other storm of nature. A tornado could never be scary again...unless it forever takes someone you love. Cars, houses and personal belongings suddenly seemed to be obsolete. And hugging our friends and family are our greatest treasures.

It was about twenty-four hours after delivering the flowers that Gary was found. He was not found on the muddy bottom of the lake as all the rescue workers had expected. But instead, just as requested, God had allowed him to be drifting, just drifting.

And when they brought him up, workers were even more shocked to see that he looked normal. Not swollen, not pale or discolored in any way, but normal…as if he were asleep.

Three days and three nights floating in the murky waters of the cold, cold lake and he looked so precious, so beautiful for his mother. It was a gift that only God could give. God had allowed the nightmare to come true in the most compassionate manner possible.

I hate the lake.

So now we gather here annually for a tournament to benefit the rescue organizations who aided in the search. A tournament in Gary's name with the sport he loved most of all; A tournament to memorialize my dear friend. A tournament I had looked forward to helping work. But the last few weeks had absorbed my thoughts and energy.

And now I was having to force myself to come. I had a dread of seeing this lake, this lake that had already taken so much and was now taking…me.

My life.

Some three weeks earlier the doctor had called to schedule surgery. It seemed the mole I'd had removed the week before had come back as a melanoma, the most deadly form of skin cancer.

"Are you serious?"

I had been in a panic for the last twenty-three years about dying of a melanoma. I had worn hats and sunscreen and most of the time wore long sleeves in the heat of the summer. I had spent countless hours as a shade seeker and was now always paranoid of having the sun shine on me for even a few seconds, much less for any long period of time.

The doctors had removed twenty-seven moles from my body over the years. Of which twelve had come back as suspicious and had to have additional excisions. I was always paranoid. I would walk into the dermatologist and announce for them to take off anything that looked remotely abnormal. I would always explain my extreme paranoia about getting a melanoma.

My mother had a melanoma and the surgery for the second excision was dreadful. They had taken out tissue roughly the size of a tennis ball. And the skin graft was even worse. She is a melanoma survivor. But still yet I had told everyone that I didn't care what I died from as long as it was not a melanoma!

But this time was different. Right before I went for the initial appointment, I was at such a peace in my relationship with God and so anxious for my Heavenly home, I told God in my prayer that it was *okay* if I died of a melanoma. I wasn't paranoid anymore. I was by no means suicidal, but it would be okay.

Whatever God wants for my life is okay. I want to live for Him. I want to be used by Him. I want to die for Him. I want to glorify Him!

But "Seriously?" The very minute I agreed that this would be okay must have been the minute that God allowed that melanoma to attack my body. I was told that it had been caught very early. And if we had waited even just a few weeks, it would have grown and spread extremely quickly. That seemed so strange to me now considering I had not been to the dermatologist in over a year.

And too when I had called to make the appointment I had complained that I was having to wait over a month to see anyone. The office had called me back with a cancellation that got me in two weeks sooner. What timing! God's timing is *always* exactly on time.

However, when I think about what in my life may have caused me to get a melanoma, it had to be when I was young. Sunburns at the beach every year were inevitable. Any time I was in the sun would almost definitely lead to a sunburn.

But the most time I had spent in the sun, the most frequent sunburns had been when I was at the lake. Hours upon hours riding up and down the lake or swimming in the lake with my shoulders at the water's surface.

I was always working so hard to get a tan because I was so fair and pale. And all I would do was burn. My shoulders, nose, chest, legs or whatever was in the sun for any length of time.

So, now as I was peering at the lake, looking out at the glistening diamonds dancing on the water's surface that I had so loved for so very long, all I could see was death and destruction. This beauty of my life was now the taker of life.

Doing what he loved had killed Levi. And doing what he loved most had killed Gary. And now, doing what I had always loved could possibly kill me.

I hate the lake. Or do I love the lake?

Oh no, I really, really hate the lake!

Jesus is Coming!

*T*HERE WAS ONE PROFOUND memory about Gary's death. It ironically was the conversations I'd had with his mother, Janet, a few months before his death.

We occasionally had lunch together and on this one incidence I had shared with her how I had been witnessing so many signs that caused me to think that the return of Christ was very near. Not just the political side of it or the fact that all of the prophetic signs in the Bible had been fulfilled, but the fact that the internet was pulling people into its web.

Strange that I would say web and yes I know they call it the web. But just as a spider draws in her victims for the kill, people are becoming increasingly dependent on the internet for life's necessities. Banks which receive and release our only means of sustenance are totally reliant on the internet now. The majority of employees are paid as direct deposit. And at an astronomical pace the root of society is funding all its expenses by automatic draft or debit and credit cards.

Just this past week I was asked about emailing employee pay stubs to them rather than giving them the paper copy. I tried to explain that this could only be done for people with email and computers. But the thought in my mind was we are forcing people into that internet dependent society.

All of this in preparation for that world currency and the mark of the beast which I think will be a computer microchip. Studies are already being conducted with these for the wealthy. And the most effective places for insertion are the wrist or the forehead, the exact locations mentioned in the Bible for the infamous mark of the beast.

Plus when I think that my parents were born into homes that didn't even have electricity, I don't know how else we could explain the technological explosion. God had for thousands of years withheld the knowledge to even make electricity. And now, in a little over a century, I'm typing on a laptop in my centrally air conditioned home as airplanes are taking off and landing within sight.

And in my lifetime I have gone from talking on a telephone, with a party line at Grandma's, to a cordless phone, to a cell phone. A cell phone which now can not only function as a phone, but as a camera, for games or to access the internet, not to mention those calculators, calendars and alarm clocks. And in all likelihood, before this book can be published, there will be additional advancements in this technological epidemic.

The rate at which advancements are accelerating is unexplainable by any other means than to admit that God has allowed this to happen now, at this precise time in history, in preparation for the return of His Precious Son, Jesus Christ.

I was so excited as I rattled on about Christ return and was so thankful for such a dear friend who shared my enthusiasm. But our conversation turned to another dear friend who was in the hospital.

Jeremy, a friend from work, had fallen onto some rocks while hiking with friends in the mountains. I shared how I had begged him not to ever hike alone again. And since I had worked there inside the national park, I knew that even the strongest of men could become a victim.

He said he would never hike alone anymore. But I had also warned him about the almost exact incidence in which he had been hurt. I had urged him passionately to never go above the water falls on those slippery rocks. But he had.

Janet shared that she did not know if she could ever recover if she lost her son, her only child. She talked on about how she thought she would probably just lose her mind if anything like that ever happened to him.

I tried to help her to see that none of us can guard our children all of the time. And I told her that I would pray that nothing would happen to Gary. But if it did that she would be at church so others could start praying for her immediately.

She questioned why God would even allow such things to happen to His Children. It would seem that these young Christian warriors should be protected with the very shields of His Hands.

So I explained that maybe God is trying to prepare the people in this area for His Coming. Maybe He is trying to reach people outside the church that He would not be able to reach otherwise.

"Okay," she agreed. "If something happens to Gary, you start praying for my sanity. And then remind me that he is only gone on before me because Jesus is coming!"

And I will be telling everyone I can,

JESUS IS COMING!

"Watch therefore, for you know neither the day nor the hour." Matthew 25:13 NKJV

"For as the lightning comes from the east and flashes to the west, so also will the coming of the Son of Man be." Matthew 24:27 NKJV

The Last Day

WHAT WOULD YOU DO IF THIS WAS THE LAST DAY OF YOUR LIFE? The question woke me like a bomb exploding in my head.

I reached for my alarm clock as it began ringing and catapulted my body out of bed. It was only six thirty and I would normally be less than coherent much less upright.

As I scrambled to take my medicine, the thought kept racing through my head, "What would I do if I knew this was going to be the last day of my life? And who had asked me this enormous question? Was God trying to tell me something?"

Frantically racing through the house getting ready for work I could barely think straight. There really was so much I would want to get done, like having my house in order. Not my spiritual house, which should be in order of course, but the actual building I live in. However with only one day, there wouldn't be time for that now!

So first I would want to see Rod and my children and my mother and my granddaughter. I would want to tell them how very much I love them. And let them know that I was sure that whatever may come, God would be watching over them. I know because He has always answered my prayers and He knows that they are permanently on the top of my list!

And there was some financial stuff I would want taken care of just to make things easier for my family. So I rushed around the house doing what I could.

The questions kept running through my mind as to whether this was really the last day of my life? Or was this God's way of helping me to get my priorities straight?

I had been thinking a lot lately about Amanda's friends Matt and Miranda. It was just three years earlier that Amanda had called me to say their mother, Donna had died. She had not been sick nor had any health problems as far as anyone knew so it had been a sudden shock.

For the year before almost weekly students had gathered at their house on Friday nights to play games, watch movies and just hang out. And when I had talked to Donna about it a few months earlier, she said she always enjoyed having the kids there.

So had God told her the day before that it was her last day on earth? Had He let her know that her final day would be soon? I knew He had let Leah's mother know.

Leah was another one of Amanda's friends whom that same year had learned that her mother had cancer. Her mother had lived long enough to see her daughter's wedding and then had gone to be with The Bridegroom.

Finally at work I couldn't think straight all day. I kept trying to have everything set for my possible, sudden departure. New instructions were quickly typed for all of the procedures and a list of passwords was left...just in case. It was really pretty exciting to think that I might soon be forever united with my Savior, my Lord and my Best Friend!

I arranged to meet all my girls for lunch and we had a wonderful time talking and laughing. I made sure when I said the blessing that I thanked God for all of these ladies whom I loved so very much. Then we all got a hug and a kiss good-bye...just in case.

Back at work I printed off some letters I had written to several people to let them know that more than anything I wanted them to know my wonderful Jesus. I called my other family and friends just to let them know I was thinking about them and that I loved them. Then finished up everything I could at work and headed home.

I tried to pay extra attention to Rod making sure he had everything he needed. Read my Bible and then off to bed for a peaceful night's sleep.

Of course, I woke up the next morning like always. "Okay, maybe yesterday was the last 'full' day of my life," I thought as I got ready for at least one more day of work. "Or…maybe there were some things I forgot to do yesterday so God's hoping I will figure it out today!"

So I jotted down some songs I would want sang at my funeral. And the list grew as the day went on. I even told one of the ministers I wanted to meet with him to ask him to sing. Thoughts raced through my head again about funeral homes, safe deposit boxes and who is going to fill out the income taxes?

Then I remembered what God had told me years ago and continues to try to demonstrate in my life. And that is to trust Him. I am still learning. But each and every day I have to set forth to do the best I can with this day…and trust Him.

This question did do one really good thing for me. Being possibly near death does make me more bold in witnessing. Where I had before feared what someone might think or do or say, I now realized I really have nothing to lose. God has held my life in His Hands all these years. And He and only He holds my future.

Soon after I came to this realization, I was pleading with God to just give me someone to tell about Jesus. Working at a church, you have to do a 'search and find' to have someone who doesn't know Jesus. And then unbeknownst to this oh-so-precious telephone survey solicitor, my prayer was answered. It was the only fun telephone survey I have ever done!

So now the question really is, "What would **you** do if this was the last day of **your** life?"

"And as it is appointed unto men once to die, but after this the judgment" Hebrews 9:27 KJV

The Bluebird

PECKING AWAY AT MY computer, there seemed to be another pecking noise coming from the parlor window. And then it would stop. And then there would be a fluttering sound against the window pane. And then it stopped again, pecking again, fluttering again, over and over.

I finally gave up, put down my computer and stomped off to the window mumbling something about "If those kids!" But as I approached the closed window blinds I could see there was a small shadow there in the very middle of the window.

Bending so quietly to peep through the blinds there was a bird. She was sitting on the window sill between the top and lower windows and was an absolutely beautiful bluebird.

However I thought at first maybe someone had a gun to her back telling her to spread eagle against the window pane. She was perched there with her wings spread full against the glass. And her head was turned sideways against the pane as if peeping with one eye in through the window blinds.

Of course when I peered through the blinds she flew away. But she landed on a leafless limb only a foot or so from the window. She looked back at me as I stared at her in disbelief.

Then as I tilted the blinds open, ever so gently to get a better look, she flew right toward me back to the window. Fluttering against the pane once more as if trying to get in and then again back to the small branch. This back and forth went on for several minutes until she finally decided that she comfortably had my undivided attention.

Next she made the long flight beneath the large, old oak tree to another leafless, low-lying limb on the other side. There she perched facing away from me beside, of all things, a dove. They were both perched side by side gazing Heavenward out over the tree tops on the other side of the driveway.

As I pondered at such an unusual sight, a bluebird and a dove on a branch together, my eyes caught sight as my ears heard the call of a cardinal. A dazzlingly red cardinal, on the center-most limb of the oak, sat perched and singing his melodious cardinal song.

"Oh!" I exclaimed, "Thank You God!" As I lifted my hands in praise, I was distracted by another bird flying in to the ground below the tree. It was a small bird with a distinct red spot on the back of its neck.

And just as it landed, another bird flew in next to it but this one was brown with a red head and neck as if wearing a red hood. The two birds pecked around on the ground in search of a delicious feast.

I could hardly believe my eyes. But just about then hopping around on the other side of the trunk of the tree was a robin. She looked very large compared to the two birds with the unusual red accents.

And then this ensemble was joined by two more friends. One was a very small, black and white bird. And the other was a very small brownish bird. At some point the female bluebird and the female cardinal had made an appearance but had quickly departed.

And yet all of the others seemed perfectly content to peck and hop along the ground beneath the tree. However, soon thereafter, the dove and the cardinal had flown away. And the bluebird had returned to the branch just in front of the window.

She continued to fly from the branch closest on the left to the branch a little farther on the right. And back and forth she flew from one side of the window to the other. And then down to a tree next to the pond. Then back to her special branch where I could admire her beauty.

At some point, overcome by the Glory of God and His creation, I began praising Him as loudly as I possibly could to make sure she could hear it. She sat ever so still on the branch gently tilting her head from side to side as if listening to the well-known melody of worship.

Then I grabbed my camera to try to get a picture of my newfound friend, but she was camera shy. She never wanted to come to the closer branch again once the camera was there. And after flying back and forth for quite a while, she eventually flew away.

As I went back to my work, my thoughts turned to why God had given me such a magnificent, wonderful sight. Only He could have orchestrated this distinguished menagerie of cordially winged creatures that had graced me with their presence.

But they kept intriguing me until I finally decided to list in order which birds I had seen. Then of course I had to look them up to determine exactly what kinds of birds had paid me this most welcomed visit. There were eight different species which seemed somewhat odd since I'd had the dream about the eight babies.

The first one and without a doubt my favorite was the bluebird which was an Eastern Bluebird. And somehow she reminded me of my precious friend Janet. And since I know she loves birds and would have loved this joyous exhibit, she just made me think of her.

But of course I knew the bird was actually the male…so maybe he reminded me of Gary. And the fact that he was a brilliant blue was so much like Gary's beautiful blue eyes. And his joyful demeanor was so very much like that gorgeous smile that everybody loved and now misses so desperately.

So the second, who sings those beautiful songs, was the dove. However, when I looked it up to get its real name which I thought was a Morning Dove, I realized it was actually a Mourning Dove. And this always eloquent, elegant bird I had constantly cherished spotting, had been singing the songs of mourning.

Now the third was even easier to identify, for it was a radiantly, bright red cardinal, a Northern Cardinal to be precise. And as I remembered him singing on that limb with all exactness in his song, he had at all times glorified the King. Therefore these two birds of song brought to mind my friends who had continued to praise God in the very midst of their mourning.

So moving on to the fourth and the fifth, there was the small bird with the red spot which I learned was a Downy Woodpecker. And since Downy always makes me think of the down on a duck, I have to think of "Duckie", Emily's nickname. And the little bird wearing the red hood was a male House Finch which immediately made me think of Lance. Thus these two tiny birds, not of the same species but only similar in size and the red markings, made me think of the tiny ones we had lost. Children whose personalities were as cheerful as the brilliant red markings were distinct.

And the sixth was the American Robin. The bird of which I am most familiar since there was always an abundance of them harvesting the sweet provisions from our backyard. Maybe sweet is a little exaggerated since I have never really tasted an earthworm.

However, for years these had been my favorite birds with their beautiful red breast so now they must remind me of some other favorite, familiar people. I was always so very fascinated as they, the robins and not the people, would hop along on the ground, feeling with their feet for the movement of their next meal.

Then the seventh and eighth would be the White-Breasted Nuthatch or maybe a Brown Creeper and the Winter Wren. Two, who were not as well-known, were there for a more hasty visit. And now less colorful and less familiar in my view of this winged sanctuary.

And just as these precious birds had feasted, entertained and taken flight from my world, so also had so many precious children. So God reminded me in those treasured moments that He watches over the birds of the air and even more so His children. And just as these birds had freedom of flight in this world, we shall soon be freed from this cage we call earth. And take flight to our Heavenly home…forevermore.

"For if He cares for all of the birds of the air, I know He'll take care of me."…"If all of the sparrows are safe and warm, we have no cause to doubt." (From We Shall See Jesus, sung April 15, 2012 at church)

"For His Eye is on the sparrow, And I know He watches me."

> *"Are not five sparrows sold for two copper coins? And not one of them is forgotten before God."* Luke 12:6 NKJV

The Final Chapter

*Y*ES, THIS IS MY final chapter. That is, this is the final chapter of my book, but the question is, "Is this the final chapter of your life?" Do you know? Does anyone know?

Therefore since your final day is actually an unknown, do you have any similar stories to share of your own? If you do, please share them with others. Let them know in whatever way you can of the wondrous joy that comes from knowing and walking with Jesus Christ. Let them know of the security you have in knowing that if you were to die today, Heaven would most definitely be your eternal home.

Your family and friends should already know who is lord of your life and where you are going when you die. There is a desperate need for people to know my wonderful Jesus. But personally, I am horrible at telling anyone myself. I am horrible at knowing how to relate to anyone the greatest message of all time. Something inside me keeps saying, "Just do it." And I want to. But instead I just continue to pray for them and nothing else. I think it was Paul who first said he did what he did not want to do and did not do what he did want to do. I am exactly that way! So instead I have resorted to writing out the stories of my life since coming to know Jesus Christ as my personal Lord and Savior.

If you don't have any stories to share, the question is why not? The answer could come from either of two reasons. First you must ask yourself, do I know Jesus Christ as my personal Savior? And is He Lord of my life? I did not ask if your name was on a church role. But instead, is there evidence of that close relationship with Jesus Christ in your life? Are you secure in knowing that Heaven is your eternal future, your eternal home?

My reasoning behind asking is simple; Rod and I were married for over five years before he was saved. We were involved in church and he was actively committed to service in the church. He was even on the church role. By all accounts, he *appeared* to be a Christian.

And yet the fact still remained that if he had died during those years, he would have gone to hell, straight to hell. Hell where the fire burns the very flesh of men for all of eternity. A real place just as real as the chair you sit in and the floor where you stand. My goal is not to scare you, but to bring you to the reality of your own eternal future. The reality that you really do not have any guarantees for your next breath or that you will wake up in the morning.

Nevertheless once Rod was truly saved, I could see the change in his life and know that at that time Jesus became Lord of his life. Rod is not perfect by any means, and no I am not going to start a list. But he has definitely changed in a way that I know could only have come from God.

The Bible tells us that Jesus warned the people that there would be those who would die *thinking* they were going to Heaven. People who had taught and told others about God, but who had never come to know Jesus Christ, had never had a personal relationship with Him. Had not trusted in Jesus as Savior or followed Him as Lord.

"Many will say to Me on that day, 'Lord, Lord, did we not prophesy in Your name, and in Your name cast out demons, and in Your name perform many miracles? And then I will declare to them, 'I never knew you. Depart from Me, you who practice lawlessness!" Matthew 7:22-23 NASB

"I never knew you. Depart from Me" are words that scare me for anyone who does not know and follow Jesus Christ as Lord. Do you know Jesus? Have you trusted Him? Is He Lord of your life?

"Depart from me, all you who do iniquity." Psalm 6:8 NASB

"A perverse heart shall depart from me; I will know no evil." Psalm 101:4 NASB

"Depart from me, evildoers." Psalm 119:115 NASB

"Then He will also say to those on His left, 'Depart from Me, accursed ones, into the eternal fire which has been prepared for the devil and his angels" Matthew 25:41 NASB

"Then He will answer and say to you, 'I do not know where you are from.' Then you will begin to say, 'We ate and drank in Your presence and You taught in our streets.' And He will say, 'I tell you, I do not know where you are from; Depart from Me, all you evildoers. In that place there will be weeping and gnashing of teeth." Luke 13:25-28 NASB

The very words of Jesus warn us of the saddest words some will ever hear, *"I do not know you. Depart from Me."* Do not think you can wait to accept and follow Him. You must answer His plea now.

"For God so loved the world that He gave His one and only Son, that whoever believes in Him shall not perish but have eternal life." John 3:16 NIV

Everlasting life with no sorrow, no pain and no fear while amidst all of the greatest of things we know on this earth plus so much more that we cannot even imagine. Or an endless, torturous termination in the very pits of hell, alone in the burning darkness in the ever painful clutches of death. The choice is yours and yours alone. God has provided in His Son your ransom. Your actual gift of life, a life grander than you can imagine for a period longer than you can calculate or ever fathom. What is your choice? Have you chosen Him?

If you do know Him, however, you may not have any stories to share simply because you have not been paying close attention. Has God been speaking and you have not been listening? Have you prayed for anything and failed to praise God for His provision? How many times have you actually claimed His Word? Or maybe I should ask, how many times have you actually *read* His Word? If you ever want to see and hear God in your life, you only have to look and listen. Sometimes we try to make things too complicated when God has already provided us with everything we need.

He has given us the Bible as a handbook for life. Read it every day in whatever way, shape or form you can. Write out or print off key verses you know you will need to remind yourself of what He is teaching you. Memorize any and all the verses you can possibly manage to absorb. If any verse is too difficult to understand, you can skip over it to what you do understand and come back to it later. If it is something you truly need to know for this season in your life, trust God to reveal that to you. He can…He really can!

And of course you can always ask Him for whatever you need. Prayer is the greatest gift God has left for us. Jesus opened the direct line to the Father for each and everyone. We can now have unlimited calling twenty-four seven to the very Creator of everything. The One who actually knows us better than we know ourselves; the One who loves us unconditionally while knowing all of our faults and shortcomings.

God wants us to come to Him with not only our biggest problems, but all of our concerns. He wants to hear from us when we are happy as well as when we are sad. He wants to hear us lifting His Name in praise. And He wants to hear us crying out to Him when we are hurting. He really wants to be everything to us that a father wants to be to that newborn baby. He wants us to totally depend on Him. To trust Him and to give Him all the admiration and respect that the most revered father deserves.

And "Pray without ceasing" I Thessalonians 5:17 NASB So pray when you wake up. Pray when you eat. Pray when you walk, or ride, or drive. Talking to God should be an open conversation, as if He were right there with you throughout the day...Isn't He? I certainly hope so. I hope that you know Jesus Christ as your Savior and He is Lord of your life. I pray that you know Him and know where you will spend your eternity.

> *"And just as each person is destined to die once and after that comes judgment, so also Christ died once for all times as a sacrifice to take away the sins of many people."* Hebrews 9:27-28 NLT

But each person has to make the decision personally for themselves. Each person has to decide whether to accept Christ or to reject Christ, once and for always.

Furthermore there is an urgency of reaching all people with His Love. The vital need is to reach people before Christ return, His imminent return.

> *"Behold, I am coming quickly!"* Revelation 3:11 NKJV

> *"Behold, I am coming quickly!"* Revelation 22:7 NKJV

> *"And behold, I am coming quickly,"* Revelation 22:12 NKJV

"Surely I am coming quickly." Revelation 22:20 NKJV

Do you think He wants us to know that He is coming quickly? Faster than the speed of light…He comes.

"He will come again, not to deal with our sins, but to bring salvation to all who are eagerly waiting for Him." Hebrews 9:28 NLT

Yes, He **will** come again. And salvation will **only** come for those who have accepted Him as their Savior and Lord. Christ will return to rescue all of the babies and children and all of those who have accepted Him. And the only ones that will be left here on this earth are those who have rejected Him. If you have never accepted Christ, then you have rejected Christ. If you are not rescued, then you will be doomed.

And as long as I am still on this earth, I never want to stand again by the casket at a funeral and wonder if this person knows my wonderful Jesus, if their eternity is in Heaven or hell. Please ask yourself that question now and decide this very moment where **you** would be if **you** were the one who had died.

Jesus is calling.

"Trust in the Lord with all your heart,
And lean not on your own understanding;
In all your ways acknowledge Him,
And He shall direct your paths."
Proverbs 3:5-6 NKJV

About the Cover Picture

THE COVER PICTURE I painted years ago as what I imagined the view was from my mother's yard as a little girl. The wood rail fence would have been built by her father. And the rose bush would have been planted by her mother, who had died before I was born. But the new life she had planted lives on. The scenery was beautiful, joyous and peaceful. Now remember, this is not what it actually looked like but what I imagined.

And of course, like my painting, there were imperfections. In painting I have always found that I am continuously trying to recreate a vision of the perfections of the Creator. And like with His creation, I am always messing it up...or should I say we. We try to cover up or hide our mistakes, in paintings and in life, even though to a true artist they are quite obvious.

At first glance of my picture, and at my life, it does look rather lovely. However the imperfections are still there and are immediately an eyesore for the paintings creator. But unlike my painting, the Creator of my life is not drawn to my own imperfections. For my flaws, my mess-ups, and all of my imperfections have been washed away by His Son. Jesus Christ has bathed me in His Love so that when God looks upon me, He only sees perfection. He only sees a beautiful, joyous and peaceful child of the King.

So although this is not a famous, artistic rendition of the view from my mother's old home place, it is the view I would like to see...

H*On My Way*ome

About the Author

GLENDA COUNTS FINLEY HAS served her Lord and Savior as the treasurer, the organist and most recently as a finance director, among other positions in His Church. She passionately loves Jesus Christ. Praising Him and bringing Him glory are her life goals.

She has always loved working for His Church. One sign she has displayed is three large letters J O Y which she will gladly tell you represent how we can have real joy in our lives, "Always keep Jesus first, Others second and Yourself last."

Glenda lives with her husband Rod in Maryville, Tennessee in the foothills of the Great Smoky Mountains National Park. Their home sits next door to her mother's on the family farm once belonging to her father, grandfather and great-grandfather. They have two daughters, Amanda and Jennifer, two sons-in-law, Robbie and Parker, and a granddaughter, Caroline, who all live there on the family farm as well. At home, Glenda enjoys reading, her Bible is her favorite, crafting, swimming and rocking her granddaughter, but rocking her granddaughter is the best!

Afterword

*T*HERE IS A PICTURE I made and hangs in my office. A sign of sorts which reads, "The tithe is the Lord's. Leviticus 27:30" Except it doesn't just say "The tithe is the Lord's" one time. It has this quote from scripture listed numerous times.

Each quote is listed in a different font. And the quotes are of different sizes. Some are very serious looking fonts. And some are more relaxed looking fonts. Some are bold and some are in italics.

And then at the bottom of the picture, in a very small font reads the last of the verse, "…it is holy to the Lord." So the tithe *is* holy to the Lord. And the tithe *is* the Lord's!

I made this sign to remind us, to remind that department, but mostly to remind me that the tithes, all of the churches finances, are God's. And that means that whether people give it or don't give it, it is His. It is His because He said it is His. And it is holy to Him.

In reality, we would have no tenth of anything if He did not give us life. And regardless of how invincible we may think we are, death is only one breath away.

Now back to the sign, the different sizes and different fonts are to remind us that regardless of whether it is coming or going, big or small, special or not so special, it is the Lord's. The tithe is the Lord's...period. The tithe is holy to the Lord...period.

"And all the tithe of the land...is the Lord's. It is holy to the Lord." Leviticus 27:30 NKJV

Notes from the Author

*I*LOVE HATS. SOME PEOPLE call me the Hat Lady because I wear hats so much. I have winter hats and summer hats. I have beach hats and funeral hats. There are wool hats and straw hats. And paper hats and polyester hats.

I have pink hats, blue hats, brown hats and white hats. And of course there are black hats and then some more pink hats. Pink is my favorite color.

Every time I wear a hat out someone will comment on how pretty it is. Then they will tell me how very much they like hats but never wear them. I wonder if they know that wearing a hat is not illegal? I think that perhaps the constitution even clearly states that all men and women in the United States have the right to wear hats.

Most people will tell me that the reason they don't wear hats is that they don't want to mess up their hair. Sometimes I want to tell them that their hair really shouldn't determine if they are having a bad day, so why not accentuate it!

Or they don't want to make a spectacle of themselves. So they must think my display of head wear is by some means an exhibition of extravagance. However, men have for years worn hats to keep their heads warm or shielded. So are they really that much smarter than women?

The truth is I started wearing hats to keep my head warm as well. This in reality kept me from getting sinus infections and ear infections. Then trying to avoid skin cancer, which obviously was only delayed, the wide brimmed hats became my forte.

So at times I think I resemble that crazy, eccentric woman that would make an interesting character in a children's book. And since I just realized that my favorite pink hat is made of paper, which is made from wood, does that make me a blockhead?

Yes, I am enjoying poking fun at myself and hope you get a giggle too from some favorite 'hat' memory. And regardless of whether people may think I'm a blockhead or a crazy, eccentric old lady, I know that God loves me,

hats and all.

"O God the Lord, the strength of my salvation, You have covered my head in the day of battle." Psalm 140:7 NKJV

And every day I am on this earth, I am in the battle against the evils of hell. Thank You, O Lord, for covering my head with all of these wonderful hats! I love you!